Real-Time Communication with WebRTC

Salvatore Loreto and Simon Pietro Romano

Beijing · Cambridge · Farnham · Köln · Sebastopol · Tokyo

Real-Time Communication with WebRTC

by Salvatore Loreto and Simon Pietro Romano

Printed in the United States of America.

Published by O'Reilly Media, Inc., 1005 Gravenstein Highway North, Sebastopol, CA 95472.

O'Reilly books may be purchased for educational, business, or sales promotional use. Online editions are also available for most titles (*http://my.safaribooksonline.com*). For more information, contact our corporate/institutional sales department: 800-998-9938 or *corporate@oreilly.com*.

Editors: Simon St.Laurent and Allyson MacDonald
Production Editor: Kristen Brown
Copyeditor: Charles Roumeliotis
Proofreader: Eliahu Sussman

Indexer: Angela Howard
Cover Designer: Karen Montgomery
Interior Designer: David Futato
Illustrator: Rebecca Demarest

May 2014:   First Edition

Revision History for the First Edition:

2014-04-15:   First release

See *http://oreilly.com/catalog/errata.csp?isbn=9781449371876* for release details.

ISBN: 978-1-449-37187-6

[LSI]

This book is dedicated to my beloved son Carmine and my wonderful wife Annalisa. They are my inspiration and motivation in everything I do.

— Salvatore Loreto

This book is dedicated to Franca (who was both my mother and my best friend) and to my beloved daughters Alice and Martina.

— Simon Pietro Romano

Table of Contents

Preface

Web Real-Time Communication (WebRTC) is a new standard that lets browsers communicate in real time using a peer-to-peer architecture. It is about secure, consent-based, audio/video (and data) peer-to-peer communication between HTML5 browsers. This is a disruptive evolution in the web applications world, since it enables, for the very first time, web developers to build real-time multimedia applications with no need for proprietary plug-ins.

WebRTC puts together two historically separated camps, associated, respectively, with telecommunications on one side and web development on the other. Those who do not come from the telecommunications world might be discouraged by the overwhelming quantity of information to be aware of in order to understand all of the nits and bits associated with real-time transmission over the Internet. On the other hand, for those who are not aware of the latest developments in the field of web programming (both client and server side), it might feel uncomfortable to move a *legacy* VoIP application to the browser.

The aim of this book is to facilitate both communities, by providing developers with a learn-by-example description of the WebRTC APIs sitting on top of the most advanced real-time communication protocols. It targets a heterogeneous readership, made not only of web programmers, but also of real-time applications architects who have some knowledge of the inner workings of the Internet protocols and communication paradigms. Different readers can enter the book at different points. They will be provided with both some theoretical explanation and a handy set of pre-tailored exercises they can properly modify and apply to their own projects.

We will first of all describe, at a high level of abstraction, the entire development cycle associated with WebRTC. Then, we will walk hand in hand with our readers and build a complete WebRTC application. We will first disregard all networking aspects related to the construction of a signaling channel between any pair of browser peers aiming to communicate. In this first phase, we will illustrate how you can write code to query (and gain access to) local multimedia resources like audio and video devices and render them within an HTML5 browser window. We will then discuss how the obtained media streams can be associated with a `PeerConnection` object representing an abstraction for a logical connection to a remote peer. During these first steps, no actual communication channel with a remote peer will be instantiated. All of the code samples will be run on a single node and will just help the programmer familiarize with the WebRTC APIs. Once done with this phase, we will briefly discuss the various choices related to the setup of a proper signaling channel allowing two peers to exchange (and negotiate) information about a real-time multimedia session between each other. For this second phase, we will unavoidably need to take a look at the server side. The running example will be purposely kept as simple as possible. It will basically represent a bare-bones piece of code focusing just on the WebRTC APIs and leave aside all stylistic aspects associated with the look and feel of the final application. We believe that readers will quickly learn how to develop their own use cases, starting from the sample code provided in the book.

The book is structured as follows:

Chapter 1, Introduction
> Covers why VoIP (Voice over IP) is shifting from standalone functionality to a browser component. It introduces the existing HTML5 features used in WebRTC and how they fit with the architectural model of real-time communication, the so-called Browser RTC Trapezoid.

Chapter 2, Handling Media in the Browser
> Focuses on the mechanisms allowing client-side web applications (typically written in a mix of HTML5 and JavaScript) to interact with web browsers through the WebRTC API. It illustrates how to query browser capabilities, receive browser-generated notifications, and apply the application-browser API in order to properly handle media in the browser.

Chapter 3, Building the Browser RTC Trapezoid: A Local Perspective
> Introduces the RTCPeerConnection API, whose main purpose is to transfer streaming data back and forth between browser peers, by providing an abstraction for a bidirectional multimedia communication channel.

Chapter 4, The Need for a Signaling Channel
> Focuses on the creation of an out-of-band signaling channel between WebRTC-enabled peers. Such a channel proves fundamental, at session setup time, in order to allow for the exchanging of both session descriptions and network reachability information.

Chapter 5, Putting It All Together: Your First WebRTC System from Scratch
> Concludes the guided WebRTC tour by presenting a complete example. The readers will learn how to create a basic yet complete Web Real-Time Communication system from scratch, using the API functionality described in the previous chapters.

Chapter 6, An Introduction to WebRTC API's Advanced Features
Explores advanced aspects of the WebRTC API and considers the future.

Conventions Used in This Book

The following typographical conventions are used in this book:

Italic
Indicates new terms, URLs, email addresses, filenames, and file extensions.

`Constant width`
Used for program listings, as well as within paragraphs to refer to program elements such as variable or function names, databases, data types, environment variables, statements, and keywords.

`Constant width bold`
Shows commands or other text that should be typed literally by the user.

`Constant width italic`
Shows text that should be replaced with user-supplied values or by values determined by context.

This element signifies a tip or suggestion.

This element signifies a general note.

This element indicates a warning or caution.

Using Code Examples

Supplemental material (code examples, exercises, etc.) is available for download at *https://github.com/spromano/WebRTC_Book*.

This book is here to help you get your job done. In general, if example code is offered with this book, you may use it in your programs and documentation. You do not need to contact us for permission unless you're reproducing a significant portion of the code. For example, writing a program that uses several chunks of code from this book does not require permission. Selling or distributing a CD-ROM of examples from O'Reilly books does require permission. Answering a question by citing this book and quoting example code does not require permission. Incorporating a significant amount of example code from this book into your product's documentation does require permission.

We appreciate, but do not require, attribution. An attribution usually includes the title, author, publisher, and ISBN. For example: "*Real-Time Communication with WebRTC* by Salvatore Loreto and Simon Pietro Romano (O'Reilly). Copyright 2014 Salvatore Loreto and Prof. Simon Pietro Romano, 978-1-449-37187-6."

If you feel your use of code examples falls outside fair use or the permission given above, feel free to contact us at *permissions@oreilly.com*.

Safari® Books Online

 *Safari Books Online* is an on-demand digital library that delivers expert content in both book and video form from the world's leading authors in technology and business.

Technology professionals, software developers, web designers, and business and creative professionals use Safari Books Online as their primary resource for research, problem solving, learning, and certification training.

Safari Books Online offers a range of product mixes and pricing programs for organizations, government agencies, and individuals. Subscribers have access to thousands of books, training videos, and prepublication manuscripts in one fully searchable database from publishers like O'Reilly Media, Prentice Hall Professional, Addison-Wesley Professional, Microsoft Press, Sams, Que, Peachpit Press, Focal Press, Cisco Press, John Wiley & Sons, Syngress, Morgan Kaufmann, IBM Redbooks, Packt, Adobe Press, FT Press, Apress, Manning, New Riders, McGraw-Hill, Jones & Bartlett, Course Technology, and dozens more. For more information about Safari Books Online, please visit us online.

How to Contact Us

Please address comments and questions concerning this book to the publisher:

O'Reilly Media, Inc.
1005 Gravenstein Highway North
Sebastopol, CA 95472
800-998-9938 (in the United States or Canada)
707-829-0515 (international or local)
707-829-0104 (fax)

We have a web page for this book, where we list errata, examples, and any additional information. You can access this page at *http://oreil.ly/realtime-comm-webRTC*.

To comment or ask technical questions about this book, send email to *bookques tions@oreilly.com*.

For more information about our books, courses, conferences, and news, see our website at *http://www.oreilly.com*.

Find us on Facebook: *http://facebook.com/oreilly*

Follow us on Twitter: *http://twitter.com/oreillymedia*

Watch us on YouTube: *http://www.youtube.com/oreillymedia*

Acknowledgments

This book wouldn't be here without the efforts of many people. The authors gratefully acknowledge some of the many here, in no particular order:

- The people at O'Reilly, with a special mention to Allyson MacDonald and Simon St.Laurent, who have enthusiastically supported our book proposal and invested considerable time and effort in bringing this manuscript to market. Allyson, in particular, has been closely involved in creating the final pages you read.

- The reviewers, who provided valuable feedback during the writing process: Lorenzo Miniero, Irene Ruengeler, Michael Tuexen, and Xavier Marjou. They all did a great job and provided us with useful hints and a thorough technical review of the final manuscript before it went to press.

- The engineers at both the IETF and the W3C who are dedicating huge efforts to making the WebRTC/RtcWeb initiatives become a reality.

- WebRTC early adopters, whose precious feedback and comments constantly help improve the specs.

CHAPTER 1

Introduction

Web Real-Time Communication (WebRTC) is a new standard and industry effort that extends the web browsing model. For the first time, browsers are able to directly exchange real-time media with other browsers in a peer-to-peer fashion.

The World Wide Web Consortium (W3C) and the Internet Engineering Task Force (IETF) are jointly defining the JavaScript APIs (Application Programming Interfaces), the standard HTML5 tags, and the underlying communication protocols for the setup and management of a reliable communication channel between any pair of next-generation web browsers.

The standardization goal is to define a WebRTC API that enables a web application running on any device, through secure access to the input peripherals (such as webcams and microphones), to exchange real-time media and data with a remote party in a peer-to-peer fashion.

Web Architecture

The classic web architecture semantics are based on a client-server paradigm, where browsers send an HTTP (Hypertext Transfer Protocol) request for content to the web server, which replies with a response containing the information requested.

The resources provided by a server are closely associated with an entity known by a URI (Uniform Resource Identifier) or URL (Uniform Resource Locator).

In the web application scenario, the server can embed some JavaScript code in the HTML page it sends back to the client. Such code can interact with browsers through standard JavaScript APIs and with users through the user interface.

WebRTC Architecture

WebRTC extends the client-server semantics by introducing a peer-to-peer communication paradigm between browsers. The most general WebRTC architectural model (see Figure 1-1) draws its inspiration from the so-called SIP (Session Initiation Protocol) Trapezoid (RFC3261).

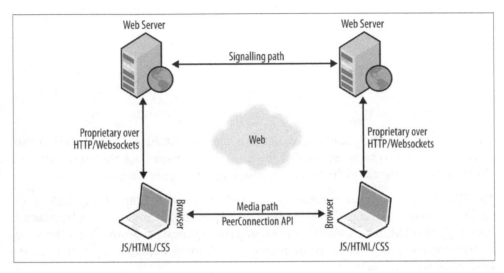

Figure 1-1. The WebRTC Trapezoid

In the WebRTC Trapezoid model, both browsers are running a web application, which is downloaded from a different web server. Signaling messages are used to set up and terminate communications. They are transported by the HTTP or WebSocket protocol via web servers that can modify, translate, or manage them as needed. It is worth noting that the signaling between browser and server is not standardized in WebRTC, as it is considered to be part of the application (see "Signaling" on page 5). As to the data path, a PeerConnection allows media to flow directly between browsers without any intervening servers. The two web servers can communicate using a standard signaling protocol such as SIP or Jingle (XEP-0166). Otherwise, they can use a proprietary signaling protocol.

The most common WebRTC scenario is likely to be the one where both browsers are running the same web application, downloaded from the same web page. In this case the Trapezoid becomes a Triangle (see Figure 1-2).

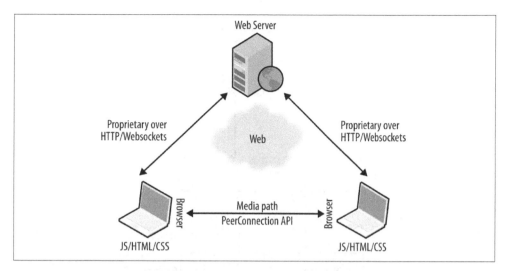

Figure 1-2. The WebRTC Triangle

WebRTC in the Browser

A WebRTC web application (typically written as a mix of HTML and JavaScript) interacts with web browsers through the standardized WebRTC API, allowing it to properly
exploit and control the real-time browser function (see Figure 1-3). The WebRTC web
application also interacts with the browser, using both WebRTC and other standardized
APIs, both proactively (e.g., to query browser capabilities) and reactively (e.g., to receive
browser-generated notifications).

The WebRTC API must therefore provide a wide set of functions, like connection management (in a peer-to-peer fashion), encoding/decoding capabilities negotiation, se-
lection and control, media control, firewall and NAT element traversal, etc.

Network Address Translator (NAT)

The Network Address Translator (NAT) (RFC1631) has been standardized to alleviate
the scarcity and depletion of IPv4 addresses.

A NAT device at the edge of a private local network is responsible for maintaining a
table mapping of private local IP and port tuples to one or more globally unique public
IP and port tuples. This allows the local IP addresses behind a NAT to be reused among
many different networks, thus tackling the IPv4 address depletion issue.

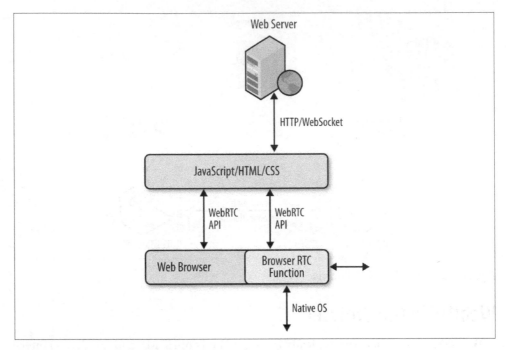

Figure 1-3. Real-time communication in the browser

The design of the WebRTC API does represent a challenging issue. It envisages that a continuous, real-time flow of data is streamed across the network in order to allow direct communication between two browsers, with no further intermediaries along the path. This clearly represents a revolutionary approach to web-based communication.

Let us imagine a real-time audio and video call between two browsers. Communication, in such a scenario, might involve direct media streams between the two browsers, with the media path negotiated and instantiated through a complex sequence of interactions involving the following entities:

- The caller browser and the caller JavaScript application (e.g., through the mentioned JavaScript API)
- The caller JavaScript application and the application provider (typically, a web server)
- The application provider and the callee JavaScript application
- The callee JavaScript application and the callee browser (again through the application-browser JavaScript API)

Signaling

The general idea behind the design of WebRTC has been to fully specify how to control the media plane, while leaving the signaling plane as much as possible to the application layer. The rationale is that different applications may prefer to use different standardized signaling protocols (e.g., SIP or eXtensible Messaging and Presence Protocol [XMPP]) or even something custom.

Session description represents the most important information that needs to be exchanged. It specifies the transport (and *Interactive Connectivity Establishment* [ICE]) information, as well as the media type, format, and all associated media configuration parameters needed to establish the media path.

Since the original idea to exchange session description information in the form of Session Description Protocol (SDP) "blobs" presented several shortcomings, some of which turned out to be really hard to address, the IETF is now standardizing the JavaScript Session Establishment Protocol (JSEP). JSEP provides the interface needed by an application to deal with the negotiated local and remote session descriptions (with the negotiation carried out through whatever signaling mechanism might be desired), together with a standardized way of interacting with the ICE state machine.

The JSEP approach delegates entirely to the application the responsibility for driving the signaling state machine: the application must call the right APIs at the right times, and convert the session descriptions and related ICE information into the defined messages of its chosen signaling protocol, instead of simply forwarding to the remote side the messages emitted from the browser.

WebRTC API

The W3C WebRTC 1.0 API allows a JavaScript application to take advantage of the novel browser's real-time capabilities. The real-time browser function (see Figure 1-3) implemented in the browser core provides the functionality needed to establish the necessary audio, video, and data channels. All media and data streams are encrypted using DTLS.[1]

---

1. DTLS is actually used for key derivation, while SRTP is used on the wire. So, the packets on the wire are not DTLS (except for the initial handshake).

Datagram Transport Layer Security (DTLS)

The DTLS (Datagram Transport Layer Security) protocol (RFC6347) is designed to prevent eavesdropping, tampering, or message forgery to the datagram transport offered by the User Datagram Protocol (UDP). The DTLS protocol is based on the stream-oriented Transport Layer Security (TLS) protocol and is intended to provide similar security guarantees.

> The DTLS handshake performed between two WebRTC clients relies on self-signed certificates. As a result, the certificates themselves cannot be used to authenticate the peer, as there is no explicit chain of trust to verify.

To ensure a baseline level of interoperability between different real-time browser function implementations, the IETF is working on selecting a minimum set of mandatory to support audio and video codecs. Opus (RFC6716) and G.711 have been selected as the mandatory to implement audio codecs. However, at the time of this writing, IETF has not yet reached a consensus on the mandatory to implement video codecs.

The API is being designed around three main concepts: MediaStream, PeerConnection, and DataChannel.

MediaStream

A MediaStream is an abstract representation of an actual stream of data of audio and/or video. It serves as a handle for managing actions on the media stream, such as displaying the stream's content, recording it, or sending it to a remote peer. A MediaStream may be extended to represent a stream that either comes from (remote stream) or is sent to (local stream) a remote node.

A LocalMediaStream represents a media stream from a local media-capture device (e.g., webcam, microphone, etc.). To create and use a local stream, the web application must request access from the user through the getUserMedia() function. The application specifies the type of media—audio or video—to which it requires access. The devices selector in the browser interface serves as the mechanism for granting or denying access. Once the application is done, it may revoke its own access by calling the stop() function on the LocalMediaStream.

Media-plane signaling is carried out of band between the peers; the Secure Real-time Transport Protocol (SRTP) is used to carry the media data together with the RTP Control Protocol (RTCP) information used to monitor transmission statistics associated with data streams. DTLS is used for SRTP key and association management.

As Figure 1-4 shows, in a multimedia communication each medium is typically carried in a separate RTP session with its own RTCP packets. However, to overcome the issue of opening a new *NAT hole* for each stream used, the IETF is currently working on the possibility of reducing the number of transport layer ports consumed by RTP-based real-time applications. The idea is to combine (i.e., *multiplex*) multimedia traffic in a single RTP session.

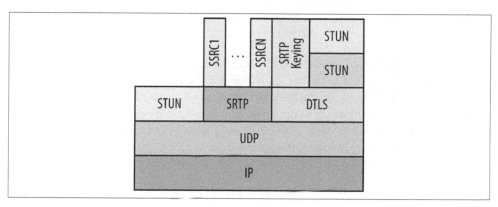

Figure 1-4. The WebRTC protocol stack

PeerConnection

A PeerConnection allows two users to communicate directly, browser to browser. It then represents an association with a remote peer, which is usually another instance of the same JavaScript application running at the remote end. Communications are coordinated via a signaling channel provided by scripting code in the page via the web server, e.g., using XMLHttpRequest or WebSocket. Once a peer connection is established, media streams (locally associated with ad hoc defined MediaStream objects) can be sent directly to the remote browser.

The `PeerConnection` mechanism uses the ICE protocol (see "ICE Candidate Exchanging" on page 117) together with the STUN and TURN servers to let UDP-based media streams traverse NAT boxes and firewalls. ICE allows the browsers to discover enough information about the topology of the network where they are deployed to find the best exploitable communication path. Using ICE also provides a security measure, as it prevents untrusted web pages and applications from sending data to hosts that are not expecting to receive them.

Each signaling message is fed into the receiving `PeerConnection` upon arrival. The APIs send signaling messages that most applications will treat as opaque blobs, but which must be transferred securely and efficiently to the other peer by the web application via the web server.

DataChannel

The DataChannel API is designed to provide a generic transport service allowing web browsers to exchange generic data in a bidirectional peer-to-peer fashion.

The standardization work within the IETF has reached a general consensus on the usage of the Stream Control Transmission Protocol (SCTP) encapsulated in DTLS to handle nonmedia data types (see Figure 1-4).

The encapsulation of *SCTP over DTLS over UDP together with ICE* provides a NAT traversal solution, as well as confidentiality, source authentication, and integrity protected transfers. Moreover, this solution allows the data transport to interwork smoothly with the parallel media transports, and both can potentially also share a single transport-layer port number. SCTP has been chosen since it natively supports multiple streams with either reliable or partially reliable delivery modes. It provides the possibility of opening several independent streams within an SCTP association towards a peering SCTP endpoint. Each stream actually represents a unidirectional logical channel providing the notion of in-sequence delivery. A message sequence can be sent either ordered or unordered. The message delivery order is preserved only for all ordered messages sent on the same stream. However, the `DataChannel` API has been designed to be bidirectional, which means that each `DataChannel` is composed as a bundle of an incoming and an outgoing SCTP stream.

The `DataChannel` setup is carried out (i.e., the SCTP association is created) when the `CreateDataChannel()` function is called for the first time on an instantiated `PeerCon nection` object. Each subsequent call to the `CreateDataChannel()` function just creates a new `DataChannel` within the existing SCTP association.

A Simple Example

Alice and Bob are both users of a common calling service. In order to communicate, they have to be simultaneously connected to the web server implementing the calling service. Indeed, when they point their browsers to the calling service web page, they will download an HTML page containing a JavaScript that keeps the browser connected to the server via a secure HTTP or WebSocket connection.

When Alice clicks on the web page button to start a call with Bob, the JavaScript instantiates a `PeerConnection` object. Once the `PeerConnection` is created, the JavaScript code on the calling service side needs to set up media and accomplishes such a task through the `MediaStream` function. It is also necessary that Alice grants permission to allow the calling service to access both her camera and her microphone.

In the current W3C API, once some streams have been added, Alice's browser, enriched with JavaScript code, generates a signaling message. The exact format of such a message has not been completely defined yet. We do know it must contain media channel information and ICE candidates, as well as a fingerprint attribute binding the communication to Alice's public key. This message is then sent to the signaling server (e.g., by XMLHttpRequest or by WebSocket).

Figure 1-5 sketches a typical call flow associated with the setup of a real-time, browser-enabled communication channel between Alice and Bob.

The signaling server processes the message from Alice's browser, determines that this is a call to Bob, and sends a signaling message to Bob's browser.

The JavaScript on Bob's browser processes the incoming message, and alerts Bob. Should Bob decide to answer the call, the JavaScript running in his browser would then instantiate a `PeerConnection` related to the message coming from Alice's side. Then, a process similar to that on Alice's browser would occur. Bob's browser verifies that the calling service is approved and the media streams are created; afterwards, a signaling message containing media information, ICE candidates, and a fingerprint is sent back to Alice via the signaling service.

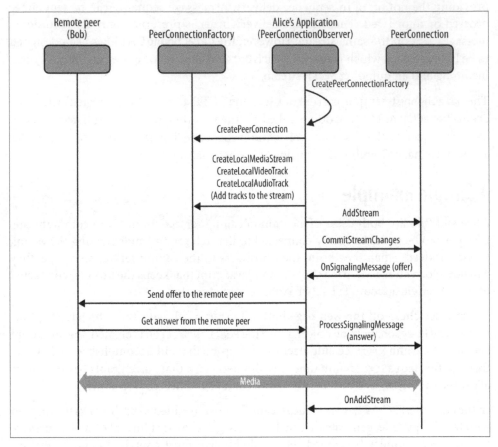

Figure 1-5. Call setup from Alice's perspective

CHAPTER 2

Handling Media in the Browser

In this chapter, we start delving into the details of the WebRTC framework, which basically specifies a set of JavaScript APIs for the development of web-based applications. The APIs have been conceived at the outset as friendly tools for the implementation of basic use cases, like a one-to-one audio/video call. They are also meant to be flexible enough to guarantee that the expert developer can implement a variegated set of much more complicated usage scenarios. The programmer is hence provided with a set of APIs which can be roughly divided into three logical groups:

1. Acquisition and management of both local and remote audio and video:

    - MediaStream interface (and related use of the HTML5 <audio> and <video> tags)

2. Management of connections:

    - RTCPeerConnection interface

3. Management of arbitrary data:

    - RTCDataChannel interface.

WebRTC in 10 Steps

The following 10-step recipe describes a typical usage scenario of the WebRTC APIs:

1. Create a MediaStream object from your local devices (e.g., microphone, webcam).
2. Obtain a *URL blob* from the local MediaStream.
3. Use the obtained URL blob for a local preview.
4. Create an RTCPeerConnection object.

5. Add the local stream to the newly created connection.

6. Send your own session description to the remote peer.

7. Receive the remote session description from your peer.

8. Process the received session description and add the remote stream to your RTCPeerConnection.

9. Obtain a URL blob from the remote stream.

10. Use the obtained URL blob to play the remote peer's audio and/or video.

We will complete the above recipe step by step. In the remainder of this chapter we will indeed cover the first three phases of the entire peer-to-peer WebRTC-based communication lifecycle. This means that we will forget about our remote peer for the moment and just focus on how to access and make use of local audio and video resources from within our browser. While doing this, we will also take a look at how to play a bit with constraints (e.g., to force video resolution).

Warning: WebRTC supported browsers

At the time of this writing, the WebRTC API is available in Chrome, Firefox, and Opera. All of the samples contained in this book have been tested with these browsers. For the sake of conciseness (and since Opera and Chrome act almost identically when it comes to the API's implementation) we will from now on just focus on Chrome and Firefox as running client platform examples.

Media Capture and Streams

The W3C *Media Capture and Streams* document defines a set of JavaScript APIs that enable the application to request audio and video streams from the platform, as well as manipulate and process the stream data.

MediaStream API

A MediaStream interface is used to represent streams of media data. Flows can be either input or output, as well as either local or remote (e.g., a local webcam or a remote connection). It has to be noted that a single MediaStream can contain zero or multiple tracks. Each track has a corresponding MediaStreamTrack object representing a specific media source in the user agent. All tracks in a MediaStream are intended to be synchronized when rendered. A MediaStreamTrack represents content comprising one or more channels, where the channels have a defined, well-known relationship to each other. A channel is the smallest unit considered in this API specification. Figure 2-1 shows a MediaStream composed of a single video track and two distinct audio (left and right channel) tracks.

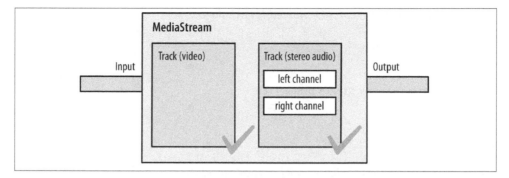

Figure 2-1. A MediaStream made of one video track and two audio tracks

The W3C *Media Capture and Streams* API defines the two methods getUserMedia() and createObjectUrl(), which are briefly explained in the following sections.

Obtaining Local Multimedia Content

The getUserMedia() API allows web developers to obtain access to local device media (currently, audio and/or video), by specifying a set of (either mandatory or optional) constraints, as well as proper callbacks for the asynchronous management of both successful and unsuccessful setup:

```
getUserMedia(constraints, successCallback, errorCallback)
```

getUserMedia() prompts the user for permission to use their webcam or other video or audio input.

URL

The createObjectUrl() method instructs the browser to create and manage a unique URL associated with either a local file or a binary object (*blob*):

```
createObjectURL(stream)
```

Its typical usage in WebRTC will be to create a blob URL starting from a MediaStream object. The blob URL will then be used inside an HTML page. This procedure is actually needed for both local and remote streams.

Playing with the getUserMedia() API

So, let's get started with the getUserMedia() API call and its returned MediaStream object. We will prepare a simple HTML page with some JavaScript code allowing us to access local video resources and display them inside an HTML5 <video> tag. Example 2-1 shows the very simple page we have built for our first example.

Example 2-1. Our first WebRTC-enabled HTML page

```
<!DOCTYPE html>
<html>
<head>

<title>getUserMedia very simple demo</title>

</head>
<body>
<div id="mainDiv">

  <h1><code>getUserMedia()</code> very simple demo</h1>

  <p>With this example, we simply call <code>getUserMedia()</code> and display
  the received stream inside an HTML5 <video> element</p>

  <p>View page source to access both HTML and JavaScript code...</p>

  <video autoplay></video>

  <script src="js/getUserMedia.js"></script>

</div>
</body>
</html>
```

Example 2-1 contains a reference to a JavaScript file (*getUserMedia.js*), whose content
is shown in Example 2-2.

Example 2-2. The getUserMedia.js file

```
// Look after different browser vendors' ways of calling the getUserMedia()
// API method:
// Opera --> getUserMedia
// Chrome --> webkitGetUserMedia
// Firefox --> mozGetUserMedia

navigator.getUserMedia = navigator.getUserMedia || navigator.webkitGetUserMedia
                         || navigator.mozGetUserMedia;

// Use constraints to ask for a video-only MediaStream:
var constraints = {audio: false, video: true};

var video = document.querySelector("video");

// Callback to be called in case of success...
function successCallback(stream) {

  // Note: make the returned stream available to console for inspection
  window.stream = stream;
```

```
  if (window.URL) {
    // Chrome case: URL.createObjectURL() converts a MediaStream to a blob URL
    video.src = window.URL.createObjectURL(stream);
  } else {
    // Firefox and Opera: the src of the video can be set directly from the stream
    video.src = stream;
  }
  // We're all set. Let's just play the video out!
  video.play();
}

// Callback to be called in case of failures...
function errorCallback(error){
  console.log("navigator.getUserMedia error: ", error);
}

// Main action: just call getUserMedia() on the navigator object
navigator.getUserMedia(constraints, successCallback, errorCallback);
```

The following screenshots show how the page looks when we load it into either Chrome (Figure 2-2) or Firefox (Figure 2-3).

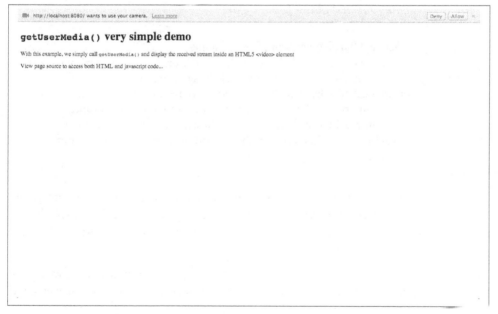

Figure 2-2. Opening our first example in Chrome

Figure 2-3. Opening our first example in Firefox

Warning: Opening JavaScript files in Chrome
If you want to test the code in Google Chrome on your local machine, you are going to face some challenges, since Chrome will not load local files by default due to security restrictions. In order to overcome such issues you'll have to either run a web server locally on your machine and use it to serve the application's files, or use the `--allow-file-access-from-files` option when launching your browser.

As you can see from the figures above, both browsers ask for the user's consent before accessing local devices (in this case, the webcam). After gathering such an explicit consent from the user, the browser eventually associates the acquired `MediaStream` with the page, as shown in Figures 2-4 and 2-5.

It is important to note that the permission grant is tied to the domain of the web page, and that this permission does not extend to pop ups and other frames on the web page.

Figure 2-4. Showing the acquired MediaStream in Chrome

Figure 2-5. Showing the acquired MediaStream in Firefox

Delving into some of the details of the simple code reported above, we can highlight how we make a call to the API method getUserMedia(constraints, successCall back, errorCallback), whose arguments have the following meaning:

- A constraints object (see "Media Constraints" on page 19), used to specify that we are interested in gathering just the local video (constraints = {audio: false, video: true}).

- A success callback which, if called, is passed a MediaStream. In our case, such a MediaStream is first made available to the console for the user's inspection (win dow.stream = stream;). Then, it is attached to the <video> element of the HTML5 page and eventually displayed. With reference to console inspection of the returned object, Figure 2-6 shows a snapshot of the output of such an activity within the developer's tool window in Chrome. Each MediaStream is characterized by a label and contains one or more MediaStreamTracks representing channels of either audio or video.

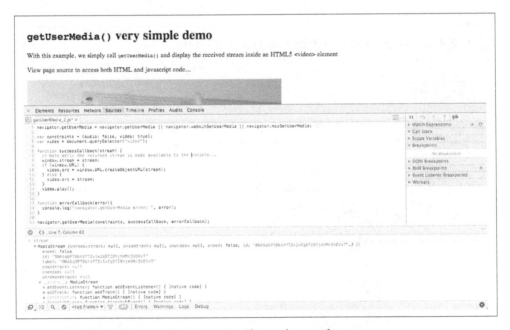

Figure 2-6. Inspecting a MediaStream in Chrome's console

With reference to how the returned stream is attached to the <video> element, notice that Chrome calls for a conversion to a so-called *blob URL* (video.src = win dow.URL.createObjectURL(stream);), whereas the other WebRTC-enabled browsers allow you to use it as is (video.src = stream;).

- A failure callback which, if called, is passed an error object. In our basic example, the mentioned callback just logs the returned error to the console (con sole.log("navigator.getUserMedia error: ", error);).

The Media Model

Browsers provide a media pipeline from sources to sinks. In a browser, sinks are the <img>, <video>, and <audio> tags. A source can be a physical webcam, a microphone, a local video or audio file from the user's hard drive, a network resource, or a static image. The media produced by these sources typically do not change over time. These sources can be considered static. The sinks that display such sources to the users (the actual tags themselves) have a variety of controls for manipulating the source content.

The getUserMedia() API method adds dynamic sources such as microphones and cameras. The caracteristics of these sources can change in response to application needs. These sources can be considered dynamic in nature.

Media Constraints

Constraints are an optional feature for restricting the range of allowed variability on a source of a MediaStream track. Constraints are exposed on tracks via the Constraina ble interface, which includes an API for dynamically changing constraints.

The getUserMedia() call also permits an initial set of constraints to be applied (for example, to set values for video resolution) when the track is first obtained.

The core concept of constraints is a *capability*, which consists of a property or feature of an object together with the set of its possible values, which may be specified either as a range or as an enumeration.

Constraints are stored on the track object, not the source. Each track can be optionally initialized with constraints. Otherwise, constraints can be added afterwards through the dedicated constraint APIs.

Constraints can be either optional or mandatory. Optional constraints are represented by an ordered list, while mandatory constraints are associated with an unordered set.

The aim is to provide support for more constraints before the final version of the API is released; such constraints will include things like aspect ratio, camera facing mode (front or back), audio and video frame rate, video height and width, and so on.

Using Constraints

In this section, we will take a quick look at how you can apply an initial set of constraints when the track is obtained using the getUserMedia() call.

Warning: `getUserMedia()` constraints support in WebRTC browsers
`getUserMedia()` constraints are currently only supported in Chrome. The example in this section will assume that you use this browser.

Let's first build the HTML page in Example 2-3.

Example 2-3. Playing with constraints: The HTML page

```
<!DOCTYPE html>
<!DOCTYPE html PUBLIC "-//W3C//DTD HTML 4.01 Transitional//EN"
        "http://www.w3.org/TR/html4/loose.dtd">
<html>
<head>

<title>getUserMedia() and constraints</title>

</head>
<body>
<div id="mainDiv">

  <h1><code>getUserMedia()</code>: playing with video constraints</h1>

  <p>Click one of the below buttons to change video resolution...</p>

    <div id="buttons">
        <button id="qvga">320x240</button>
        <button id="vga">640x480</button>
        <button id="hd">1280x960</button>
    </div>

  <p id="dimensions"></p>

  <video autoplay></video>

  <script src="js/getUserMedia_constraints.js"></script>
</div>

</body>
</html>
```

As you can see from both the code snippet in Example 2-3 and the snapshot in Figure 2-7, the page contains three buttons, each associated with the local video stream represented at a specific resolution (from low resolution, up to high-definition video).

getUserMedia(): playing with video constraints

Click one of the below buttons to change video resolution...

320x240px   640x480px   1280x960px

Figure 2-7. A simple HTML page showing the use of constraints in Chrome

Example 2-4 shows the JavaScript code used to both acquire the local video stream and attach it to the web page with a well-defined resolution.

Example 2-4. Playing with constraints: The getUserMedia_constraints.js file

```
// Define local variables associated with video resolution selection
// buttons in the HTML page
var vgaButton = document.querySelector("button#vga");
var qvgaButton = document.querySelector("button#qvga");
var hdButton = document.querySelector("button#hd");

// Video element in the HTML5 page
var video = document.querySelector("video");

// The local MediaStream to play with
var stream;

// Look after different browser vendors' ways of calling the
// getUserMedia() API method:
navigator.getUserMedia = navigator.getUserMedia ||
  navigator.webkitGetUserMedia || navigator.mozGetUserMedia;

// Callback to be called in case of success...
function successCallback(gotStream) {
  // Make the stream available to the console for introspection
  window.stream = gotStream;
```

```
  // Attach the returned stream to the <video> element
  // in the HTML page
  video.src = window.URL.createObjectURL(stream);

  // Start playing video
  video.play();
}

// Callback to be called in case of failure...
function errorCallback(error){
  console.log("navigator.getUserMedia error: ", error);
}

// Constraints object for low resolution video
var qvgaConstraints  = {
  video: {
    mandatory: {
      maxWidth: 320,
      maxHeight: 240
    }
  }
};

// Constraints object for standard resolution video
var vgaConstraints  = {
  video: {
    mandatory: {
      maxWidth: 640,
      maxHeight: 480
    }
  }
};

// Constraints object for high resolution video
var hdConstraints  = {
  video: {
    mandatory: {
      minWidth: 1280,
      minHeight: 960
    }
  }
};

// Associate actions with buttons:
qvgaButton.onclick = function(){getMedia(qvgaConstraints)};
vgaButton.onclick = function(){getMedia(vgaConstraints)};
hdButton.onclick = function(){getMedia(hdConstraints)};


// Simple wrapper for getUserMedia() with constraints object as
// an input parameter
function getMedia(constraints){
```

```
if (!!stream) {
  video.src = null;
  stream.stop();
}
navigator.getUserMedia(constraints, successCallback, errorCallback);
}
```

The code in Example 2-4 is quite straightforward. The core part is related to the proper definition of constraints objects, each of which can be passed as an input parameter to the getUserMedia() function. The three sample objects therein contained simply state that video is to be considered mandatory and further specify resolution in terms of lower bounds on both its width and height. To give the reader a flavor of what this means, Figures 2-8 and 2-9 show, respectively, a 320×240 and a 640×480 resolution stream.

Figure 2-8. Showing 320×240 resolution video in Chrome

Figure 2-9. Showing 640×480 resolution video in Chrome

CHAPTER 3

Building the Browser RTC Trapezoid: A Local Perspective

In the previous chapter, we started to delve into the details of the *Media Capture and Streams* API by covering the first three steps of what we called a 10-step web real-time communications recipe. In particular, we discussed a couple of examples showing how we can access and manage local media streams by using the `getUserMedia()` method. The time is now ripe to start taking a look at the *communication* part.

In this chapter we will analyze the *WebRTC 1.0* API, whose main purpose is to allow media to be sent to and received from another browser.

As we already anticipated in previous chapters, a mechanism is needed to properly coordinate the real-time communication, as well as to let peers exchange control messages. Such a mechanism, universally known as *signaling*, has not been defined inside WebRTC and thus does not belong in the RTCPeerConnection API specification.

The choice to make such an API agnostic with respect to signaling was made at the outset. Signaling is not standardized in WebRTC because the interoperability between browsers is ensured by the web server, using downloaded JavaScript code. This means that WebRTC developers can implement the signaling channel by relying on their favorite messaging protocol (SIP, XMPP, Jingle, etc.), or they can design a proprietary signaling mechanism that might only provide the features needed by the application.

The one and only architectural requirement with respect to this part of a WebRTC application concerns the availability of a properly configured bidirectional communication channel between the web browser and the web server. XMLHttpRequest (XHR), WebSocket, and solutions like Google's Channel API represent good candidates for this.

The signaling channel is needed to allow the exchange of three types of information between WebRTC peers:

Media session management
    Setting up and tearing down the communication, as well as reporting potential error conditions

Nodes' network configuration
    Network addresses and ports available for the exchanging of real-time data, even in the presence of NATs

Nodes' multimedia capabilities
    Supported media, available encoders/decoders (*codecs*), supported resolutions and frame rates, etc.

No data can be transferred between WebRTC peers before all of the above information has been properly exchanged and negotiated.

In this chapter, we will disregard all of the above mentioned issues related to the setup (and use) of a signaling channel and just focus on the description of the RTCPeerConnection API. We will achieve this goal by somehow emulating peer-to-peer behavior on a single machine. This means that we will for the time being bypass the signaling channel setup phase and let the three steps mentioned above (session management, network configuration, and multimedia capabilities exchange) happen on a single machine. In Chapter 5 we will eventually add the last brick to the WebRTC building, by showing how the local scenario can become a distributed one thanks to the introduction of a real signaling channel between two WebRTC-enabled peers.

Coming back to the API, calling new `RTCPeerConnection` (configuration) creates an `RTCPeerConnection` object, which is an abstraction for a communication channel between two users/browsers and can be either input or output for a particular `Media Stream`, as illustrated in Figure 3-1. The `configuration` parameter contains information to find access to the STUN and TURN servers, necessary for the NAT traversal setup phase.

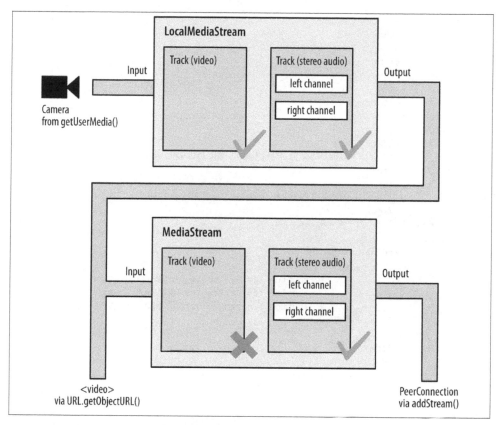

Figure 3-1. Adding a MediaStream to a PeerConnection

Using PeerConnection Objects Locally: An Example

Let's now start with the simple HTML code shown in Example 3-1.

Example 3-1. Local RTCPeerConnection usage example

```
<!DOCTYPE html PUBLIC "-//W3C//DTD HTML 4.01 Transitional//EN"
        "http://www.w3.org/TR/html4/loose.dtd">
<html>

<head>

<title>Local PeerConnection() example</title>

</head>

<body>

<table border="1" width="100%">
```

```
        <tr>
                <th>
                        Local video
                </th>
                <th>
                        'Remote' video
                </th>
        </tr>
        <tr>
                <td>
                        <video id="localVideo" autoplay></video>
                </td>
                <td>
                        <video id="remoteVideo" autoplay></video>
                </td>
        </tr>
        <tr>
                <td align="center">
                        <div>
                                <button id="startButton">Start</button>
                                <button id="callButton">Call</button>
                                <button id="hangupButton">Hang Up</button>
                        </div>

                </td>
                <td>
                        <!-- void -->
                </td>
        </tr>
</table>

<script src="js/localPeerConnection.js"></script>

</body>

</html>
```

Example 3-1 acts as a container for two video streams, represented side by side in a table
format. The stream on the left represents a local capture, whereas the one on the right
mimics a remote party (which will actually be a further capture of the local audio and
video devices). Media capture and rendering is triggered by events associated with three
buttons, which function, respectively, to start the application, to place a call between
the local and the (fake) remote party, and to hang up the call. The core of this application
is, as usual, the JavaScript code contained in the file *localPeerConnection.js*, which is
reported in the following:

```
// JavaScript variables holding stream and connection information
var localStream, localPeerConnection, remotePeerConnection;

// JavaScript variables associated with HTML5 video elements in the page
var localVideo = document.getElementById("localVideo");
```

```
var remoteVideo = document.getElementById("remoteVideo");

// JavaScript variables assciated with call management buttons in the page
var startButton = document.getElementById("startButton");
var callButton = document.getElementById("callButton");
var hangupButton = document.getElementById("hangupButton");

// Just allow the user to click on the Call button at start-up
startButton.disabled = false;
callButton.disabled = true;
hangupButton.disabled = true;

// Associate JavaScript handlers with click events on the buttons
startButton.onclick = start;
callButton.onclick = call;
hangupButton.onclick = hangup;

// Utility function for logging information to the JavaScript console
function log(text) {
  console.log("At time: " + (performance.now() / 1000).toFixed(3) + " --> " \
              + text);
}

// Callback in case of success of the getUserMedia() call
function successCallback(stream){
  log("Received local stream");

  // Associate the local video element with the retrieved stream
  if (window.URL) {
    localVideo.src = URL.createObjectURL(stream);
  } else {
    localVideo.src = stream;
  }

  localStream = stream;

  // We can now enable the Call button
  callButton.disabled = false;
}

// Function associated with clicking on the Start button
// This is the event triggering all other actions
function start() {
  log("Requesting local stream");
  // First of all, disable the Start button on the page
  startButton.disabled = true;
  // Get ready to deal with different browser vendors...
  navigator.getUserMedia = navigator.getUserMedia ||
    navigator.webkitGetUserMedia || navigator.mozGetUserMedia;
  // Now, call getUserMedia()
  navigator.getUserMedia({audio:true, video:true}, successCallback,
    function(error) {
```

```
          log("navigator.getUserMedia error: ", error);
    });
}


// Function associated with clicking on the Call button
// This is enabled upon successful completion of the Start button handler
function call() {
  // First of all, disable the Call button on the page...
  callButton.disabled = true;
  // ...and enable the Hangup button
  hangupButton.disabled = false;
  log("Starting call");

  // Note that getVideoTracks() and getAudioTracks() are not currently
  // supported in Firefox...
  // ...just use them with Chrome
  if (navigator.webkitGetUserMedia) {
        // Log info about video and audio device in use
        if (localStream.getVideoTracks().length > 0) {
          log('Using video device: ' + localStream.getVideoTracks()[0].label);
        }
        if (localStream.getAudioTracks().length > 0) {
          log('Using audio device: ' + localStream.getAudioTracks()[0].label);
        }
  }

  // Chrome
  if (navigator.webkitGetUserMedia) {
        RTCPeerConnection = webkitRTCPeerConnection;
  // Firefox
  } else if(navigator.mozGetUserMedia){
        RTCPeerConnection = mozRTCPeerConnection;
        RTCSessionDescription = mozRTCSessionDescription;
        RTCIceCandidate = mozRTCIceCandidate;
  }
  log("RTCPeerConnection object: " + RTCPeerConnection);

  // This is an optional configuration string, associated with
  // NAT traversal setup
  var servers = null;

  // Create the local PeerConnection object
  localPeerConnection = new RTCPeerConnection(servers);
  log("Created local peer connection object localPeerConnection");
  // Add a handler associated with ICE protocol events
  localPeerConnection.onicecandidate = gotLocalIceCandidate;

  // Create the remote PeerConnection object
  remotePeerConnection = new RTCPeerConnection(servers);
  log("Created remote peer connection object remotePeerConnection");
  // Add a handler associated with ICE protocol events...
```

```
    remotePeerConnection.onicecandidate = gotRemoteIceCandidate;
    // ...and a second handler to be activated as soon as the remote
    // stream becomes available.
    remotePeerConnection.onaddstream = gotRemoteStream;

    // Add the local stream (as returned by getUserMedia())
    // to the local PeerConnection.
    localPeerConnection.addStream(localStream);
    log("Added localStream to localPeerConnection");

    // We're all set! Create an Offer to be 'sent' to the callee as soon
    // as the local SDP is ready.
    localPeerConnection.createOffer(gotLocalDescription, onSignalingError);
}

function onSignalingError(error){
    console.log('Failed to create signaling message : ' + error.name);
}

// Handler to be called when the 'local' SDP becomes available
function gotLocalDescription(description){
    // Add the local description to the local PeerConnection
    localPeerConnection.setLocalDescription(description);
    log("Offer from localPeerConnection: \n" + description.sdp);

    // ...do the same with the 'pseudoremote' PeerConnection
    // Note: this is the part that will have to be changed if you want
    // the communicating peers to become remote
    // (which calls for the setup of a proper signaling channel)
    remotePeerConnection.setRemoteDescription(description);

    // Create the Answer to the received Offer based on the 'local' description
    remotePeerConnection.createAnswer(gotRemoteDescription, onSignalingError);
}

// Handler to be called when the remote SDP becomes available
function gotRemoteDescription(description){
    // Set the remote description as the local description of the
    // remote PeerConnection.
    remotePeerConnection.setLocalDescription(description);
    log("Answer from remotePeerConnection: \n" + description.sdp);
    // Conversely, set the remote description as the remote description of the
    // local PeerConnection
    localPeerConnection.setRemoteDescription(description);
}

// Handler to be called when hanging up the call
function hangup() {
    log("Ending call");
    // Close PeerConnection(s)
    localPeerConnection.close();
    remotePeerConnection.close();
```

```
      // Reset local variables
      localPeerConnection = null;
      remotePeerConnection = null;
      // Disable Hangup button
      hangupButton.disabled = true;
      // Enable Call button to allow for new calls to be established
      callButton.disabled = false;
    }

    // Handler to be called as soon as the remote stream becomes available
    function gotRemoteStream(event){
      // Associate the remote video element with the retrieved stream
      if (window.URL) {
        // Chrome
        remoteVideo.src = window.URL.createObjectURL(event.stream);
      } else {
        // Firefox
        remoteVideo.src = event.stream;
      }
      log("Received remote stream");
    }

    // Handler to be called whenever a new local ICE candidate becomes available
    function gotLocalIceCandidate(event){
      if (event.candidate) {
          // Add candidate to the remote PeerConnection
        remotePeerConnection.addIceCandidate(new RTCIceCandidate(event.candidate));
        log("Local ICE candidate: \n" + event.candidate.candidate);
      }
    }

    // Handler to be called whenever a new remote ICE candidate becomes available
    function gotRemoteIceCandidate(event){
      if (event.candidate) {
          // Add candidate to the local PeerConnection
        localPeerConnection.addIceCandidate(new RTCIceCandidate(event.candidate));
        log("Remote ICE candidate: \n " + event.candidate.candidate);
      }
    }
```

In order to easily understand the contents of this code, let's follow the evolution of our application step by step. We will show screen captures taken with both Chrome and Firefox, so you can appreciate the differences related to both the look and feel of the application and the developers' tools made available by the two browsers.

Starting the Application

Here is what happens when the user clicks on the Start button in Chrome (Figure 3-2) and in Firefox (Figure 3-3).

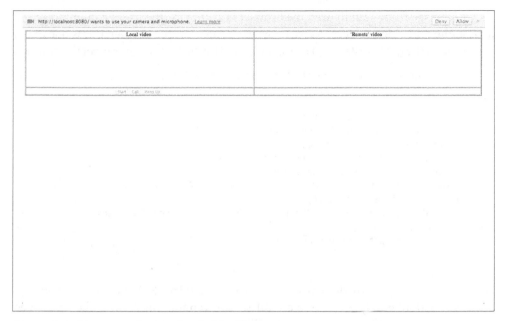

Figure 3-2. The example page loaded in Chrome

Figure 3-3. The example page loaded in Firefox

As you can see from both figures, the browser is asking for the user's consent to access local audio and video devices. As we know from the previous chapter, this is due to the execution of the getUserMedia() call, as indicated by the JavaScript snippet that follows:

```
// Function associated with clicking on the Start button
// This is the event triggering all other actions
function start() {
  log("Requesting local stream");
  // First of all, disable the Start button on the page
  startButton.disabled = true;
  // Get ready to deal with different browser vendors...
  navigator.getUserMedia = navigator.getUserMedia ||
    navigator.webkitGetUserMedia || navigator.mozGetUserMedia;
  // Now, call getUserMedia()
  navigator.getUserMedia({audio:true, video:true}, successCallback,
    function(error) {
      log("navigator.getUserMedia error: ", error);
    });
}
```

As soon as the user provides consent, the successCallback() function is triggered. Such a function simply attaches the local stream (containing both audio and video tracks) to the localVideo element in the HTML5 page:

```
...
// Associate the local video element with the retrieved stream
if (window.URL) {
    localVideo.src = URL.createObjectURL(stream);
} else {
        localVideo.src = stream;
}

localStream = stream;
...
```

The effect of the execution of the callback is shown in Figure 3-4 (Chrome) and Figure 3-5 (Firefox).

Figure 3-4. The example page after user grants consent, in Chrome

Figure 3-5. The example page after user grants consent, in Firefox

Placing a Call

Once consent has been granted, the Start button gets disabled and the Call button becomes in turn enabled. If the user clicks on it, the Call() function is triggered. Such a function first does some basic housekeeping like disabling the Call button and enabling the Hangup button. Then, in the case of Chrome and Opera (this feature is not currently implemented in Firefox), it logs some information about the available media tracks to the console:

```
// Function associated with clicking on the Call button
// This is enabled upon successful completion of the Start button handler
function call() {
    // First of all, disable the Call button on the page...
    callButton.disabled = true;
    // ...and enable the Hangup button
    hangupButton.disabled = false;
    log("Starting call");

    // Note that getVideoTracks() and getAudioTracks() are not currently
    // supported in Firefox...
    // ...just use them with Chrome
    if (navigator.webkitGetUserMedia) {
        // Log info about video and audio device in use
            if (localStream.getVideoTracks().length > 0) {
              log('Using video device: ' + localStream.getVideoTracks()[0].label);
            }
            if (localStream.getAudioTracks().length > 0) {
              log('Using audio device: ' + localStream.getAudioTracks()[0].label);
            }
    }
    ...
```

The getVideoTracks() and getAudioTracks() methods, defined by the MediaStream constructor in the Media Capture and Streams API, return a sequence of MediaStreamTrack objects representing, respectively, the video tracks and the audio tracks in the stream.

Once done with the preceding operations, we finally get into the core of the code, namely the part where we encounter the RTCPeerConnection object for the very first time:

```
...
// Chrome
 if (navigator.webkitGetUserMedia) {
     RTCPeerConnection = webkitRTCPeerConnection;
 // Firefox
 } else if(navigator.mozGetUserMedia){
         RTCPeerConnection = mozRTCPeerConnection;
         RTCSessionDescription = mozRTCSessionDescription;
         RTCIceCandidate = mozRTCIceCandidate;
```

```
        }
        log("RTCPeerConnection object: " + RTCPeerConnection);
        ...
```

The above snippet contains some JavaScript code that has a solitary goal of detecting the type of browser in use, in order to give the right name to the right object. You will notice from the code that the standard RTCPeerConnection object is currently prefixed both in Chrome (webkitRTCPeerConnection) and in Firefox (mozRTCPeerConnection). The latter browser, by the way, also has a nonstandard way of naming the related RTCSessionDescription and RTCIceCandidate objects associated, respectively, with the description of the session to be negotiated and the representation of ICE protocol candidate addresses (see Chapter 4).

Once the (right) RTCPeerConnection object has been identified, we can eventually instantiate it:

```
        ...
        // This is an optional configuration string, associated with
        // NAT traversal setup
        var servers = null;

        // Create the local PeerConnection object
        localPeerConnection = new RTCPeerConnection(servers);
        log("Created local peer connection object localPeerConnection");
        // Add a handler associated with ICE protocol events
        localPeerConnection.onicecandidate = gotLocalIceCandidate;
        ...
```

The above snippet shows that an RTCPeerConnection object is instantiated through a constructor taking an optional servers parameter as input. Such a parameter can be used to properly deal with NAT traversal issues, as will be explained in Chapter 4.

RTCPeerConnection

Calling new RTCPeerConnection(configuration) creates an RTCPeerConnection object. The configuration has the information to find and access the STUN and TURN servers (there may be multiple servers of each type, with any TURN server also acting as a STUN server). Optionally, it also takes a MediaConstraints object "Media Constraints" on page 19.

When the RTCPeerConnection constructor is invoked, it also creates an ICE Agent responsible for the ICE state machine, controlled directly by the browser. The ICE Agent will proceed with gathering the candidate addresses when the IceTransports constraint is not set to "none."

An RTCPeerConnection object has two associated stream sets. A *local streams set*, representing streams that are currently sent, and a *remote streams set*, representing streams

---

that are currently received through this `RTCPeerConnection` object. The stream sets are initialized to empty sets when the `RTCPeerConnection` object is created.

The interesting thing to notice here is that the configuration of the newly created `Peer Connection` is done asynchronously, through the definition of proper callback methods.

The `onicecandidate` handler is triggered whenever a new candidate is made available to the local peer by the ICE protocol machine inside the browser.

```
// Handler to be called whenever a new local ICE candidate becomes available
function gotLocalIceCandidate(event){
  if (event.candidate) {
    // Add candidate to the remote PeerConnection
    remotePeerConnection.addIceCandidate(new RTCIceCandidate(event.candidate));
    log("Local ICE candidate: \n" + event.candidate.candidate);
  }
}
```

The `addIceCandidate()` method provides a remote candidate to the ICE Agent. In addition to being added to the remote description, connectivity checks will be sent to the new candidates as long as the `IceTransports` constraint is not set to "none."

The snippet takes for granted that the remote peer is actually run locally, which avoids the need for sending information about the gathered local address to the other party across a properly configured signaling channel. Here is why this application won't work at all if you try and run it on two remote machines. In subsequent chapters we will discuss how we can create such a signaling channel and use it to transfer ICE-related (as well as session-related) information to the remote party. For the moment, we simply add the gathered local network reachability information to the (locally available) *remote peer connection*. Clearly, the same reasoning applies when switching roles between caller and callee, i.e., the remote candidates will simply be added to the *local peer connection* as soon as they become available:

```
...
// Create the remote PeerConnection object
remotePeerConnection = new RTCPeerConnection(servers);
log("Created remote peer connection object remotePeerConnection");
// Add a handler associated with ICE protocol events...
remotePeerConnection.onicecandidate = gotRemoteIceCandidate;
// ...and a second handler to be activated as soon as the remote
// stream becomes available
```

```
remotePeerConnection.onaddstream = gotRemoteStream;
...
```

 The onaddstream and onremovestream handlers are called any time a MediaStream is respectively added or removed by the remote peer. Both will be fired only as a result of the execution of the setRemote Description() method.

The preceding snippet is related to the onaddstream handler, whose implementation looks after attaching the remote stream (as soon as it becomes available) to the remote Video element of the HTML5 page, as reported in the following:

```
// Handler to be called as soon as the remote stream becomes available
function gotRemoteStream(event){
    // Associate the remote video element with the retrieved stream
    if (window.URL) {
        // Chrome
        remoteVideo.src = window.URL.createObjectURL(event.stream);
    } else {
      // Firefox
        remoteVideo.src = event.stream;
    }
    log("Received remote stream");
}
```

Coming back to the Call() function, the only remaining actions concern adding the local stream to the local PeerConnection and eventually invoking the createOffer() method on it:

```
...
// Add the local stream (as returned by getUserMedia())
// to the local PeerConnection
  localPeerConnection.addStream(localStream);
log("Added localStream to localPeerConnection");

// We're all set! Create an Offer to be 'sent' to the callee as soon as
// the local SDP is ready
localPeerConnection.createOffer(gotLocalDescription,onSignalingError);
}

function onSignalingError(error) {
    console.log('Failed to create signaling message : ' + error.name);
}
```

 The addStream() and removeStream() methods add a stream to and remove a stream from an RTCPeerConnection object, respectively.

The createOffer() method plays a fundamental role, since it asks the browser to properly examine the internal state of the PeerConnection and generate an appropriate RTCSessionDescription object, thus initiating the Offer/Answer-state machine.

 The createOffer() method generates an SDP blob containing an RFC3264 offer with the supported configurations for the session: the descriptions of the local MediaStreams attached, the codec/RTP/RTCP options supported by the browser, and any candidates that have been gathered by the ICE Agent. The constraints parameter may be supplied to provide additional control over the offer generated.

The createOffer() method takes as input a callback (gotLocalDescription) to be called as soon as the session description is made available to the application. Also in this case, once the session description is available, the local peer should send it to the callee by using the signaling channel. For the moment, we will skip this phase and once more make the assumption that the remote party is actually a locally reachable one, which translates to the following actions:

```
// Handler to be called when the 'local' SDP becomes available
function gotLocalDescription(description){
    // Add the local description to the local PeerConnection
    localPeerConnection.setLocalDescription(description);
    log("Offer from localPeerConnection: \n" + description.sdp);

    // ...do the same with the 'pseudoremote' PeerConnection
    // Note: this is the part that will have to be changed if
    // you want the communicating peers to become remote
    // (which calls for the setup of a proper signaling channel)
    remotePeerConnection.setRemoteDescription(description);

    // Create the Answer to the received Offer based on the 'local' description
    remotePeerConnection.createAnswer(gotRemoteDescription,onSignalingError);
}
```

As stated in the commented snippet above, we herein directly set the retrieved session description as both the local description for the local peer and the remote description for the remote peer.

 The setLocalDescription() and setRemoteDescription() methods instruct the RTCPeerConnection to apply the supplied RTCSessionDescription as the local description and as the remote offer or answer, respectively.

Then, we ask the remote peer to answer the offered session by calling the createAnswer() method on the remote peer conection. Such a method takes as input parameter a callback (`gotRemoteDescription`) to be called as soon as the remote browser makes its own session description available to the remote peer. Such a handler actually mirrors the behavior of the companion callback on the caller's side:

```
// Handler to be called when the remote SDP becomes available
function gotRemoteDescription(description){
    // Set the remote description as the local description of the
    // remote PeerConnection
    remotePeerConnection.setLocalDescription(description);
    log("Answer from remotePeerConnection: \n" + description.sdp);
    // Conversely, set the remote description as the remote description
    // of the local PeerConnection
    localPeerConnection.setRemoteDescription(description);
}
```

The `createAnswer()` method generates an SDP answer with the supported configuration for the session that is compatible with the parameters in the remote configuration.

The entire call flow described above can actually be tracked down on the browser's console, as shown in Figure 3-6 (Chrome) and Figure 3-7 (Firefox).

Figure 3-6. Chrome console tracking down a call between two local peers

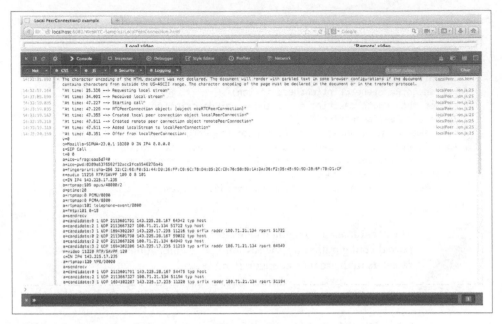

Figure 3-7. Firefox console tracking down a call between two local peers

The two snapshots show the sequence of events that have been logged by the application, as well as session description information in an SDP-compliant format. This last part of the log will become clearer when we briefly introduce the Session Description Protocol in Chapter 4.

When all of the above steps have completed, we finally see the two streams inside our browser's window, as shown in Figure 3-8 (Chrome) and Figure 3-9 (Firefox).

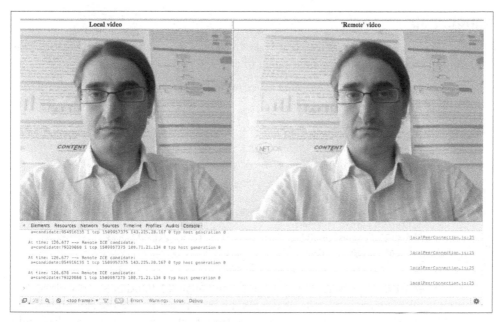

Figure 3-8. Chrome showing local and remote media after a successful call

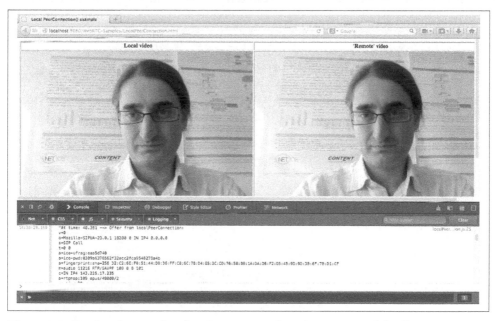

Figure 3-9. Firefox showing local and remote media after a successful call

Hanging Up

Once done with a call, the user can tear it down by clicking on the Hangup button. This triggers the execution of the associated handler:

```
// Handler to be called when hanging up the call
function hangup() {
  log("Ending call");
  // Close PeerConnection(s)
  localPeerConnection.close();
  remotePeerConnection.close();
  // Reset local variables
  localPeerConnection = null;
  remotePeerConnection = null;
  // Disable Hangup button
  hangupButton.disabled = true;
  // Enable Call button to allow for new calls to be established
  callButton.disabled = false;
}
```

As we can see from a quick look at the code, the hangup() handler simply closes the instantiated peer connections and releases resources. It then disables the Hangup button and enables the Call button, thus rolling the settings back to the point we reached right after starting the application for the very first time (i.e., after the getUserMedia() call). We're now in a state from which a new call can be placed and the game can be started all over again. This situation is depicted in Figure 3-10 (Chrome) and Figure 3-11 (Firefox).

The close() method destroys the RTCPeerConnection ICE Agent, abruptly ending any active ICE processing and any active streams, and releasing any relevant resources.

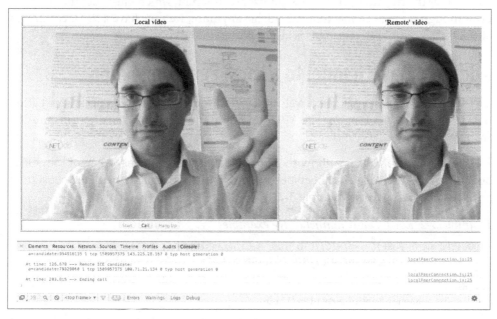

Figure 3-10. Chrome after tearing down a call

Figure 3-11. Firefox after tearing down a call

Notice that the two frames in both windows are different, which illustrates the fact that, even though no peer connection is available anymore, we now have a *live* local stream and a *frozen* remote stream. This is also reported in the console log.

Adding a DataChannel to a Local PeerConnection

The Peer-to-Peer Data API lets a web application send and receive generic application data in a peer-to-peer fashion. The API for sending and receiving data draws inspiration from WebSocket.

In this section we will show how to add a `DataChannel` to a `PeerConnection`. Once again, we will stick to the local perspective and ignore signaling issues. Let's get started with the HTML5 page in Example 3-2.

Example 3-2. Local DataChannel usage example

```
<!DOCTYPE html PUBLIC "-//W3C//DTD HTML 4.01 Transitional//EN"
          "http://www.w3.org/TR/html4/loose.dtd">
<html>
<head>
<title>DataChannel simple example</title>
</head>

<body>
    <textarea rows="5" cols="50" id="dataChannelSend" disabled placeholder="
              1: Press Start; 2: Enter text; 3: Press Send."></textarea>
        <textarea rows="5" cols="50" id="dataChannelReceive" disabled></textarea>

  <div id="buttons">
    <button id="startButton">Start</button>
    <button id="sendButton">Send</button>
    <button id="closeButton">Stop</button>
  </div>

<script src="js/dataChannel.js"></script>

</body>
</html>
```

The page (whose look and feel in Chrome is illustrated in Figure 3-12) simply contains two side-by-side text areas associated, respectively, with data to be sent from the sender's data channel, and data received by the other party on the receiver's data channel. Three buttons are used to orchestrate the application: (1) a Start button to be pressed upon startup; (2) a Send button to be used whenever new data has to be streamed across the data channel; and (3) a Close button useful for resetting the application and bringing it back to its original state.

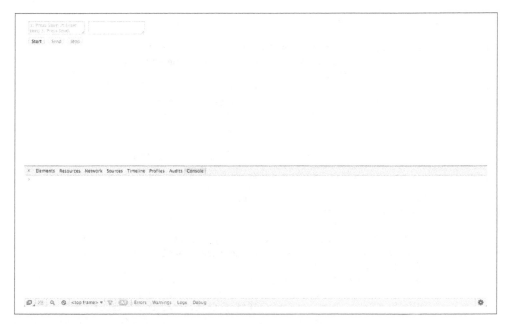

Figure 3-12. The DataChannel example page loaded in Chrome

As usual, the core behavior of this application is implemented in the embedded Java-
Script file *dataChannel.js*, which is laid out in the following:

```
//JavaScript variables associated with send and receive channels
var sendChannel, receiveChannel;

//JavaScript variables associated with demo buttons
var startButton = document.getElementById("startButton");
var sendButton = document.getElementById("sendButton");
var closeButton = document.getElementById("closeButton");

//On startup, just the Start button must be enabled
startButton.disabled = false;
sendButton.disabled = true;
closeButton.disabled = true;

//Associate handlers with buttons
startButton.onclick = createConnection;
sendButton.onclick = sendData;
closeButton.onclick = closeDataChannels;

//Utility function for logging information to the JavaScript console
function log(text) {
    console.log("At time: " + (performance.now() / 1000).toFixed(3) +
            " --> " + text);
}
```

```
function createConnection() {
        // Chrome
        if (navigator.webkitGetUserMedia) {
                RTCPeerConnection = webkitRTCPeerConnection;
                // Firefox
        } else if(navigator.mozGetUserMedia){
                RTCPeerConnection = mozRTCPeerConnection;
                RTCSessionDescription = mozRTCSessionDescription;
                RTCIceCandidate = mozRTCIceCandidate;
        }
        log("RTCPeerConnection object: " + RTCPeerConnection);

        // This is an optional configuration string
// associated with NAT traversal setup
        var servers = null;

        // JavaScript variable associated with proper
        // configuration of an RTCPeerConnection object:
        // use DTLS/SRTP
        var pc_constraints = {
                        'optional': [
                                        {'DtlsSrtpKeyAgreement': true}
                                        ]};

        // Create the local PeerConnection object...
        // ...with data channels
        localPeerConnection = new RTCPeerConnection(servers,pc_constraints);

        log("Created local peer connection object, with Data Channel");


        try {
                // Note: SCTP-based reliable DataChannels supported
                // in Chrome 29+ !
                // use {reliable: false} if you have an older version of Chrome
                sendChannel = localPeerConnection.createDataChannel( \
                                "sendDataChannel",{reliable: true});
                log('Created reliable send data channel');
        } catch (e) {
                alert('Failed to create data channel!');
                log('createDataChannel() failed with following message: ' \
                + e.message);
        }
        // Associate handlers with peer connection ICE events
        localPeerConnection.onicecandidate = gotLocalCandidate;

        // Associate handlers with data channel events
        sendChannel.onopen = handleSendChannelStateChange;
        sendChannel.onclose = handleSendChannelStateChange;

        // Mimic a remote peer connection
        window.remotePeerConnection = new RTCPeerConnection(servers, \
```

```
        pc_constraints);
        log('Created remote peer connection object, with DataChannel');

        // Associate handlers with peer connection ICE events...
        remotePeerConnection.onicecandidate = gotRemoteIceCandidate;
        // ...and data channel creation event
        remotePeerConnection.ondatachannel = gotReceiveChannel;

        // We're all set! Let's start negotiating a session...
        localPeerConnection.createOffer(gotLocalDescription,onSignalingError);

        // Disable Start button and enable Close button
        startButton.disabled = true;
        closeButton.disabled = false;
}

function onSignalingError(error) {
        console.log('Failed to create signaling message : ' + error.name);
}

// Handler for sending data to the remote peer
function sendData() {
        var data = document.getElementById("dataChannelSend").value;
        sendChannel.send(data);
        log('Sent data: ' + data);
}

// Close button handler
function closeDataChannels() {
        // Close channels...
        log('Closing data channels');
        sendChannel.close();
        log('Closed data channel with label: ' + sendChannel.label);
        receiveChannel.close();
        log('Closed data channel with label: ' + receiveChannel.label);
        // Close peer connections
        localPeerConnection.close();
        remotePeerConnection.close();
        // Reset local variables
        localPeerConnection = null;
        remotePeerConnection = null;
        log('Closed peer connections');
        // Rollback to the initial setup of the HTML5 page
        startButton.disabled = false;
        sendButton.disabled = true;
        closeButton.disabled = true;
        dataChannelSend.value = "";
        dataChannelReceive.value = "";
        dataChannelSend.disabled = true;
        dataChannelSend.placeholder = "1: Press Start; 2: Enter text; \
                                      3: Press Send.";
}
```

```
// Handler to be called as soon as the local SDP is made available to
// the application
function gotLocalDescription(desc) {
        // Set local SDP as the right (local/remote) description for both local
        // and remote parties
        localPeerConnection.setLocalDescription(desc);
        log('localPeerConnection\'s SDP: \n' + desc.sdp);
        remotePeerConnection.setRemoteDescription(desc);

        // Create answer from the remote party, based on the local SDP
        remotePeerConnection.createAnswer(gotRemoteDescription,onSignalingError);
}

// Handler to be called as soon as the remote SDP is made available to
// the application
function gotRemoteDescription(desc) {
        // Set remote SDP as the right (remote/local) description for both local
        // and remote parties
        remotePeerConnection.setLocalDescription(desc);
        log('Answer from remotePeerConnection\'s SDP: \n' + desc.sdp);
        localPeerConnection.setRemoteDescription(desc);
}

// Handler to be called whenever a new local ICE candidate becomes available
function gotLocalCandidate(event) {
        log('local ice callback');
        if (event.candidate) {
                remotePeerConnection.addIceCandidate(event.candidate);
                log('Local ICE candidate: \n' + event.candidate.candidate);
        }
}

// Handler to be called whenever a new remote ICE candidate becomes available
function gotRemoteIceCandidate(event) {
        log('remote ice callback');
        if (event.candidate) {
                localPeerConnection.addIceCandidate(event.candidate);
                log('Remote ICE candidate: \n ' + event.candidate.candidate);
        }
}

// Handler associated with the management of remote peer connection's
// data channel events
function gotReceiveChannel(event) {
        log('Receive Channel Callback: event --> ' + event);
        // Retrieve channel information
        receiveChannel = event.channel;

        // Set handlers for the following events:
        // (i) open; (ii) message; (iii) close
        receiveChannel.onopen = handleReceiveChannelStateChange;
```

```
            receiveChannel.onmessage = handleMessage;
            receiveChannel.onclose = handleReceiveChannelStateChange;
}

// Message event handler
function handleMessage(event) {
        log('Received message: ' + event.data);
        // Show message in the HTML5 page
        document.getElementById("dataChannelReceive").value = event.data;
        // Clean 'Send' text area in the HTML page
        document.getElementById("dataChannelSend").value = '';
}

// Handler for either 'open' or 'close' events on sender's data channel
function handleSendChannelStateChange() {
        var readyState = sendChannel.readyState;
        log('Send channel state is: ' + readyState);
        if (readyState == "open") {
                // Enable 'Send' text area and set focus on it
                dataChannelSend.disabled = false;
                dataChannelSend.focus();
                dataChannelSend.placeholder = "";
                // Enable both Send and Close buttons
                sendButton.disabled = false;
                closeButton.disabled = false;
        } else { // event MUST be 'close', if we are here...
                // Disable 'Send' text area
                dataChannelSend.disabled = true;
                // Disable both Send and Close buttons
                sendButton.disabled = true;
                closeButton.disabled = true;
        }
}

// Handler for either 'open' or 'close' events on receiver's data channel
function handleReceiveChannelStateChange() {
        var readyState = receiveChannel.readyState;
        log('Receive channel state is: ' + readyState);
}
```

As we did with the previous example, we will analyze the behavior of the application by following its lifecycle step by step. We will skip all those parts that have already been explained. This allows us to focus just on the new functionality introduced in the code.

Starting Up the Application

When the user clicks on the Start button in the page, a number of events happen behind the scenes. Namely, the createConnection() handler is activated. Such a handler creates both the local and the (fake) remote peer connections, in much the same way as we saw with the previous example. The difference here is that this time, the peer connection is also equipped with a data channel for the streaming of generic data:

```
...
  // JavaScript variable associated with proper
    // configuration of an RTCPeerConnection object:
    // use DTLS/SRTP
    var pc_constraints = {
                    'optional': [
                                {'DtlsSrtpKeyAgreement': true}
                                ]};

    // Create the local PeerConnection object...
    // ...with data channels
    localPeerConnection = new RTCPeerConnection(servers,pc_constraints);

    log("Created local peer connection object, with DataChannel");


    try {
            // Note: SCTP-based reliable data channels supported
            // in Chrome 29+ !
            // use {reliable: false} if you have an older version of Chrome
            sendChannel = localPeerConnection.createDataChannel( \
                    "sendDataChannel", {reliable: true});
            log('Created reliable send data channel');
    } catch (e) {
            alert('Failed to create data channel!');
            log('createDataChannel() failed with following message: ' \
            + e.message);
    }
...
```

The preceding snippet shows how to add a `DataChannel` to an existing `PeerConnec`
`tion` by calling the `createDataChannel()` method. Note that this is a browser-specific
feature, not a standardized constraint.

 The WebRTC API does not define the use of constraints with the
DataChannel API. It instead defines the usage of the so-called
`RTCDataChannelInit` dictionary (Table 3-1).

The data channel itself is actually added to the newly instantiated peer connection by
calling the `createDataChannel("sendDataChannel", {reliable: true});` method
on it. The code shows that such a data channel can be either unreliable or reliable.
Reliability is guaranteed by the proper use of the SCTP protocol and is a feature that
has been initially made available just in Firefox. Is has only recently been implemented
in Chrome (since version 29 of the browser).

createDataChannel

The createDataChannel() method creates a new RTCDataChannel object with the given label. The RTCDataChannelInit dictionary (Table 3-1) can be used to configure properties of the underlying channel, such as data reliability.

The RTCDataChannel interface represents a bidirectional data channel between two peers. Each data channel has an associated underlying data transport that is used to transport data to the other peer. The properties of the underlying data transport are configured by the peer as the channel is created (Table 3-1). The properties of a channel cannot change after the channel has been created. The actual wire protocol between the peers is SCTP (see "DataChannel" on page 8).

An RTCDataChannel can be configured to operate in different reliability modes. A reliable channel ensures that data is delivered to the other peer through retransmissions. An unreliable channel is configured to either limit the number of retransmissions (maxRetransmits) or set a time during which retransmissions are allowed (maxRetransmitTime). These properties cannot be used simultaneously and an attempt to do so will result in an error. Not setting any of these properties results in the creation of a reliable channel.

Table 3-1. RTCDataChannelInit dictionary members

Member	Type	Description
id	unsigned short	Overrides the default selection of id for this channel.
maxRetransmits	unsigned short	Limits the number of times a channel will retransmit data if not successfully delivered.
maxRetransmitTime	unsigned short	Limits the time during which the channel will retransmit data if not successfully delivered.
negotiated	boolean	The default value of false tells the user agent to announce the channel in-band and instruct the other peer to dispatch a corresponding RTCDataChannel object.
ordered	boolean	If set to false, data are allowed to be delivered out of order. The default value of true guarantees that data will be delivered in order.
protocol	DOMString	Subprotocol name used for this channel.

Local data channel events (onopen and onclose) are dealt with through proper handlers, as illustrated in the following:

```
...
// Associate handlers with send data channel events
sendChannel.onopen = handleSendChannelStateChange;
sendChannel.onclose = handleSendChannelStateChange;
...
```

As to the remote data channel (ondatachannel), it also evolves through events and related callbacks:

```
...
remotePeerConnection.ondatachannel = gotReceiveChannel;
...
```

This callback is actually activated as soon as the pseudosignaling phase successfully completes. Such a phase is triggered by the call `localPeerConnection.createOff er(gotLocalDescription,onSignalingError)`, which initiates the aforementioned call flow involving the gathering of ICE protocol candidates, as well as the exchanging of session descriptions.

The annotations on the JavaScript console log in Figures 3-13 and 3-14 show the first phases of the bootstrapping procedure, as it takes place in Chrome and in Firefox, respectively. We can see from the logs that the Offer/Answer phase starts right after the creation of the local and remote peer connections.

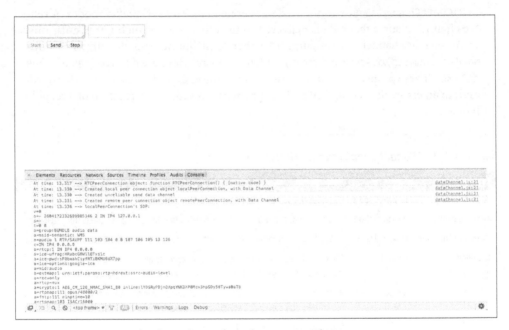

Figure 3-13. Starting the data channel application in Chrome

Figure 3-14. Starting the data channel application in Firefox

The answer, in particular, is prepared as soon as the local SDP is made available to the application, inside the `gotLocalDescription()` handler:

```
function gotLocalDescription(desc) {
  // Set local SDP as the right (local/remote) description for both local
  // and remote parties
  localPeerConnection.setLocalDescription(desc);
  log('localPeerConnection\'s SDP: \n' + desc.sdp);
  remotePeerConnection.setRemoteDescription(desc);

  // Create answer from the remote party, based on the local SDP
  remotePeerConnection.createAnswer(gotRemoteDescription,onSignalingError);
}
```

Data channel state changes are dealt with, respectively, through the `handleSendChan nelStateChange()` and `handleReceiveChannelStateChange()` event handlers. Upon reception of the open event, the former function prepares the HTML5 page for editing inside the sender's text area, at the same time enabling both the Send and the Close buttons:

```
  ...
  if (readyState == "open") {
    // Enable 'Send' text area and set focus on it
    dataChannelSend.disabled = false;
    dataChannelSend.focus();
    dataChannelSend.placeholder = "";
```

```
        // Enable both Send and Close buttons
    sendButton.disabled = false;
    closeButton.disabled = false;
    ...
```

On the receiver's side, the state change handler just logs information to the JavaScript console:

```
function handleReceiveChannelStateChange() {
    var readyState = receiveChannel.readyState;
    log('Receive channel state is: ' + readyState);
}
```

The snapshots in Figure 3-15 (Chrome) and Figure 3-16 (Firefox) show the application's state at the end of the bootstrapping procedure.

Figure 3-15. The data channel application in Chrome, after startup

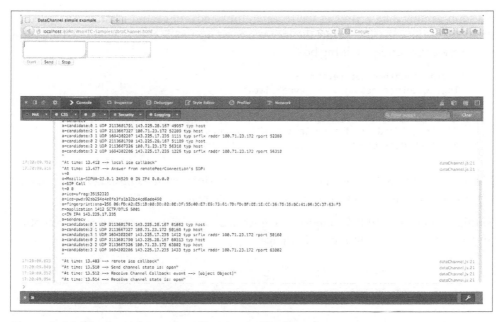

Figure 3-16. The data channel application in Firefox, after startup

Streaming Text Across the Data Channel

Once the data channel is ready, we can finally use it to transfer information between the sender and the receiver. Indeed, the user can edit a message inside the sender's text area and then click on the Send button in order to stream such information across the already instantiated data channel, by using the sendData() handler:

```
function sendData() {
  var data = document.getElementById("dataChannelSend").value;
  sendChannel.send(data);
  log('Sent data: ' + data);
}
```

The send() method attempts to send data on the channel's underlying data transport.

As soon as new data arrives at the receiver, the handleMessage() handler is called in turn. Such a handler first prints the received message inside the receiver's text area and then resets the sender's editing box:

```
function handleMessage(event) {
  log('Received message: ' + event.data);
  // Show message in the HTML5 page
  document.getElementById("dataChannelReceive").value = event.data;
  // Clean 'Send' text area in the HTML page
  document.getElementById("dataChannelSend").value = '';
}
```

Figures 3-17 and 3-18 show the application's state right before a message is transferred across the data channel in Chrome and in Firefox, respectively.

Similarly, Figure 3-19 (Chrome) and Figure 3-20 (Firefox) report message reception and associated actions in the HTML page.

Figure 3-17. Getting ready to stream a message across the data channel in Chrome

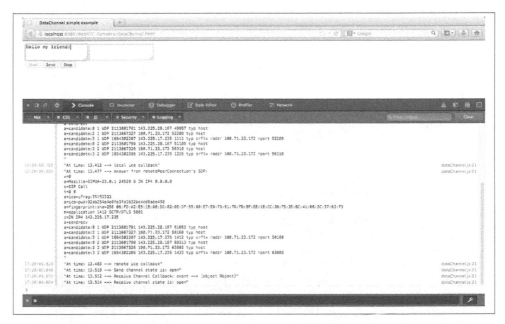

Figure 3-18. Getting ready to stream a message across the data channel in Firefox

Figure 3-19. Receiving a message from the data channel in Chrome

Figure 3-20. Receiving a message from the data channel in Firefox

Closing the Application

Once done with data transfers, the user can click on the Close button in order to:

- Close the data channels:

```
function closeDataChannels() {
  // Close channels...
  log('Closing data channels');
  sendChannel.close();
  log('Closed data channel with label: ' + sendChannel.label);
  receiveChannel.close();
  log('Closed data channel with label: ' + receiveChannel.label);
  ...
```

The close() method attempts to close the channel.

- Close the peer connections:

```
...
// Close peer connections
localPeerConnection.close();
remotePeerConnection.close();
// Reset local variables
localPeerConnection = null;
remotePeerConnection = null;
log('Closed peer connections');
...
```

- Reset the application:

```
...
// Rollback to the initial setup of the HTML5 page
startButton.disabled = false;
sendButton.disabled = true;
closeButton.disabled = true;
dataChannelSend.value = "";
dataChannelReceive.value = "";
dataChannelSend.disabled = true;
dataChannelSend.placeholder = "1: Press Start; 2: Enter text;
3: Press Send.";
}
```

By looking at both the HTML page and JavaScript console in Figure 3-21 (Chrome) and Figure 3-22 (Firefox), the reader can appreciate the effect of the execution of this code.

Figure 3-21. Closing channels and resetting the application in Chrome

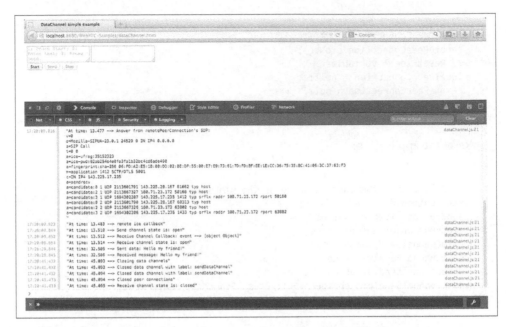

Figure 3-22. Closing channels and resetting the application in Firefox

CHAPTER 4

The Need for a Signaling Channel

As we anticipated in Chapter 3, a signaling channel is needed in a WebRTC-enabled application in order to allow for the exchanging of both session descriptions and network reachability information. Up until now, we have disregarded this specific aspect by sticking to a local perspective. This turned out to be useful, since it allowed us to just focus on the details of the WebRTC APIs, while leaving aside all networking-related aspects. The time is now ripe to also tackle these last issues. In this chapter, we will describe how we can create a proper signaling channel between any pair of peers that are interested in successfully setting up a WebRTC-enabled communication session.

The material presented in this chapter is only loosely related to the main topic of the book. More precisely, we will herein just focus on the creation of the above-mentioned signaling channel by describing the design and implementation of a very simple Java-Script application involving two clients and a server. The example itself should provide the reader with a set of tools that can be easily reused in a wide set of application scenarios. In the following chapter we will finally put all pieces together in order to complete the 10-step WebRTC recipe in a distributed setting.

Building Up a Simple Call Flow

As usual, we will continue to embrace the learn-by-example approach in order to let you figure out how to build a server-assisted signaling channel between two remote peers. In this chapter, we will focus on the realization of a simple interaction scenario, as formally depicted in the sequence diagram in Figure 4-1.

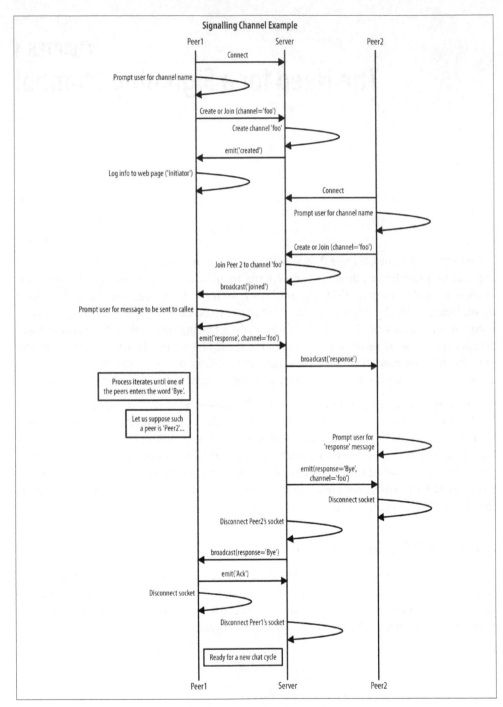

Figure 4-1. Signaling channel example: Sequence diagram

The diagram in the picture involves three different actors:

- A channel initiator, such as the peer that first takes the initiative of creating a dedicated communication channel with a remote party
- A signaling server, managing channel creation and acting as a message relaying node
- A channel *joiner*, for instance, a remote party joining an already existing channel

The idea is that the channel is created on demand by the server after receiving a specific request issued by the initiator. As soon as the second peer joins the channel, conversation can start. Message exchanging always happens through the server, which basically acts as a transparent relay node. When one of the peers decides to quit an ongoing conversation, it issues an ad hoc message (called *Bye* in the figure) towards the server, before disconnecting. This message is dispatched by the server to the remote party, which also disconnects, after having sent an acknowledgment back to the server. The receipt of the acknowledgment eventually triggers the channel reset procedure on the server's side, thus bringing the overall scenario back to its original configuration.

Let's start by building a simple HTML5 page (see Example 4-1), containing an initially empty `<div>` element which will be used to track down the evolution of the communication between two remote peers interacting through the signaling server.

Example 4-1. Simple signaling channel

```
<!DOCTYPE html PUBLIC "-//W3C//DTD HTML 4.01 Transitional//EN"
                        "http://www.w3.org/TR/html4/loose.dtd">
<html>
<head>

<title>WebRTC client</title>

</head>

<body>

<script src='/socket.io/socket.io.js'></script>

<div id="scratchPad"></div>

<script type="text/javascript" src="js/simpleNodeClient.js"></script>

</body>
</html>
```

As you can see from the HTML code, the page includes two JavaScript files. The former (*socket.io.js*) refers to the well-known `socket.io` library for real-time web applications.

The socket.io JavaScript Library

`socket.io` is a JavaScript library for real-time web applications. It has two parts: a client-side library that runs in the browser, and a server-side library for Node.js (see "The Node.js Software Platform" on page 70.)

The client-side part of `socket.io` is an event-driven library that primarily uses the WebSocket protocol, but if needed can fall back onto multiple other methods, such as *Adobe Flash sockets*, *AJAX long polling*, and others, while providing the same interface. It provides many advanced features, like associating multiple sockets with a server-side *room*, broadcasting to multiple sockets, storing data associated with specific clients, and managing asynchronous I/O.

`socket.io` can be easily installed with the *node packaged modules* (npm) tool:

```
npm install socket.io
```

Once installed, the *socket.io.js* file has to be copied to a folder where it can be found by the web server.

The demo application also requires the `node-static` module, which needs to be installed as well:

```
npm install node-static
```

The latter file (*simpleNodeClient.js*) is presented in the following:

```
// Get <div> placeholder element from DOM
div = document.getElementById('scratchPad');

// Connect to server
var socket = io.connect('http://localhost:8181');

// Ask channel name from user
channel = prompt("Enter signaling channel name:");

if (channel !== "") {
    console.log('Trying to create or join channel: ', channel);
    // Send 'create or join' to the server
    socket.emit('create or join', channel);
}


// Handle 'created' message
socket.on('created', function (channel){
        console.log('channel ' + channel + ' has been created!');
        console.log('This peer is the initiator...');
```

```javascript
        // Dynamically modify the HTML5 page
        div.insertAdjacentHTML( 'beforeEnd', '<p>Time: ' +
                (performance.now() / 1000).toFixed(3) + ' --> Channel '
                + channel + ' has been created! </p>');

        div.insertAdjacentHTML( 'beforeEnd', '<p>Time: ' +
                (performance.now() / 1000).toFixed(3) +
                ' --> This peer is the initiator...</p>');
});


// Handle 'full' message
socket.on('full', function (channel){
        console.log('channel ' + channel + ' is too crowded! \
                Cannot allow you to enter, sorry :-(');

        div.insertAdjacentHTML( 'beforeEnd', '<p>Time: ' +
                (performance.now() / 1000).toFixed(3) + ' --> \
        channel ' + channel + ' is too crowded! \
                Cannot allow you to enter, sorry :-( </p>');
});

// Handle 'remotePeerJoining' message
socket.on('remotePeerJoining', function (channel){
        console.log('Request to join ' + channel);
        console.log('You are the initiator!');

        div.insertAdjacentHTML( 'beforeEnd', '<p style="color:red">Time: ' +
                (performance.now() / 1000).toFixed(3) +
                ' --> Message from server: request to join channel ' +
                channel + '</p>');
});

// Handle 'joined' message
socket.on('joined', function (msg){
        console.log('Message from server: ' + msg);

        div.insertAdjacentHTML( 'beforeEnd', '<p>Time: ' +
                (performance.now() / 1000).toFixed(3) +
                ' --> Message from server: </p>');
        div.insertAdjacentHTML( 'beforeEnd', '<p style="color:blue">' +
                msg + '</p>');

        div.insertAdjacentHTML( 'beforeEnd', '<p>Time: ' +
                (performance.now() / 1000).toFixed(3) +
                ' --> Message from server: </p>');
        div.insertAdjacentHTML( 'beforeEnd', '<p style="color:blue">' +
                msg + '</p>');
});

// Handle 'broadcast: joined' message
socket.on('broadcast: joined', function (msg){
```

```
        div.insertAdjacentHTML( 'beforeEnd', '<p style="color:red">Time: ' +
                (performance.now() / 1000).toFixed(3) +
                ' --> Broadcast message from server: </p>');
        div.insertAdjacentHTML( 'beforeEnd', '<p style="color:red">' +
                msg + '</p>');

        console.log('Broadcast message from server: ' + msg);

        // Start chatting with remote peer:
        // 1. Get user's message
        var myMessage = prompt('Insert message to be sent to your peer:', "");

        // 2. Send to remote peer (through server)
        socket.emit('message', {
                channel: channel,
                message: myMessage});
});

// Handle remote logging message from server
socket.on('log', function (array){
        console.log.apply(console, array);
});

// Handle 'message' message
socket.on('message', function (message){
        console.log('Got message from other peer: ' + message);

        div.insertAdjacentHTML( 'beforeEnd', '<p>Time: ' +
                (performance.now() / 1000).toFixed(3) +
                ' --> Got message from other peer: </p>');
        div.insertAdjacentHTML( 'beforeEnd', '<p style="color:blue">' +
                message + '</p>');

        // Send back response message:
        // 1. Get response from user
        var myResponse = prompt('Send response to other peer:', "");

        // 2. Send it to remote peer (through server)
        socket.emit('response', {
                channel: channel,
                message: myResponse});

});

// Handle 'response' message
socket.on('response', function (response){
        console.log('Got response from other peer: ' + response);

        div.insertAdjacentHTML( 'beforeEnd', '<p>Time: ' +
                (performance.now() / 1000).toFixed(3) +
                ' --> Got response from other peer: </p>');
```

```
        div.insertAdjacentHTML( 'beforeEnd', '<p style="color:blue">' +
                response + '</p>');

        // Keep on chatting
        var chatMessage = prompt('Keep on chatting. \
        Write "Bye" to quit conversation', "");

        // User wants to quit conversation: send 'Bye' to remote party
        if(chatMessage == "Bye"){
                div.insertAdjacentHTML( 'beforeEnd', '<p>Time: ' +
                        (performance.now() / 1000).toFixed(3) +
                        ' --> Sending "Bye" to server...</p>');
                console.log('Sending "Bye" to server');

                socket.emit('Bye', channel);

                div.insertAdjacentHTML( 'beforeEnd', '<p>Time: ' +
                        (performance.now() / 1000).toFixed(3) +
                        ' --> Going to disconnect...</p>');
                console.log('Going to disconnect...');

                // Disconnect from server
                socket.disconnect();
        }else{
                // Keep on going: send response back
                // to remote party (through server)
                socket.emit('response', {
                        channel: channel,
                        message: chatMessage});
        }
});

// Handle 'Bye' message
socket.on('Bye', function (){
        console.log('Got "Bye" from other peer! Going to disconnect...');

        div.insertAdjacentHTML( 'beforeEnd', '<p>Time: ' +
                (performance.now() / 1000).toFixed(3) +
                ' --> Got "Bye" from other peer!</p>');

        div.insertAdjacentHTML( 'beforeEnd', '<p>Time: ' +
                (performance.now() / 1000).toFixed(3) +
                ' --> Sending "Ack" to server</p>');

        // Send 'Ack' back to remote party (through server)
        console.log('Sending "Ack" to server');

        socket.emit('Ack');

        // Disconnect from server
        div.insertAdjacentHTML( 'beforeEnd', '<p>Time: ' +
                (performance.now() / 1000).toFixed(3) +
```

```
        ' --> Going to disconnect...</p>');
    console.log('Going to disconnect...');

    socket.disconnect();
});
```

The code performs the following actions:

1. Allows the client to connect to the server (through the `socket.io` library)
2. Prompts the user for the name of the channel she wants to join
3. Sends a `create` or `join` request to the server
4. Starts to asynchronously handle server-sent events.

In the remainder of this chapter, we will follow a complete call flow in a step-by-step fashion. Before doing this, though, we will take a look at the server-side behavior. The server has been written by leveraging the Node.js JavaScript library.

The Node.js Software Platform

Node.js (*http://www.nodejs.org*) is an extremely powerful software platform that allows users to easily build scalable server-side applications with JavaScript. It is based on a single-threaded event loop management process making use of nonblocking I/O.

The library provides a built-in HTTP server implementation, making it independent from third-party software components. With Node.js, it is really easy for the programmer to implement a high-performance HTTP server with customized behavior with just a few lines of code.

Let's go over the server-side code. It basically looks after the creation of a server instance listening on port 8181. The code allows for the creation of server-side "rooms" hosting two client sockets at most. The first client that asks for the creation of a room is the channel initiator.

After channel creation, the server-side policy is the following:

1. The second client arriving is allowed to join the newly created channel.
2. All other clients are denied access to the room (and are consequently notified of such an event).

```
var static = require('node-static');

var http = require('http');

// Create a node-static server instance listening on port 8181
var file = new(static.Server)();
```

```javascript
// We use the http module's createServer function and
// use our instance of node-static to serve the files
var app = http.createServer(function (req, res) {
  file.serve(req, res);
}).listen(8181);

// Use socket.io JavaScript library for real-time web applications
var io = require('socket.io').listen(app);

// Let's start managing connections...
io.sockets.on('connection', function (socket){

    // Handle 'message' messages
    socket.on('message', function (message) {
        log('S --> Got message: ', message);

        socket.broadcast.to(message.channel).emit('message', \
                message.message);
    });

    // Handle 'create or join' messages
    socket.on('create or join', function (channel) {
        var numClients = io.sockets.clients(channel).length;
        console.log('numclients = ' + numClients);

        // First client joining...
        if (numClients == 0){
            socket.join(channel);
            socket.emit('created', channel);
        // Second client joining...
        } else if (numClients == 1) {
        // Inform initiator...
                io.sockets.in(channel).emit('remotePeerJoining', channel);
                // Let the new peer join channel
        socket.join(channel);

        socket.broadcast.to(channel).emit('broadcast: joined', 'S --> \
            broadcast(): client ' + socket.id + ' joined channel ' \
                    + channel);
        } else { // max two clients
                console.log("Channel full!");
            socket.emit('full', channel);
        }
    });

    // Handle 'response' messages
    socket.on('response', function (response) {
        log('S --> Got response: ', response);

        // Just forward message to the other peer
        socket.broadcast.to(response.channel).emit('response',
```

```
            response.message);
    });

    // Handle 'Bye' messages
    socket.on('Bye', function(channel){
        // Notify other peer
        socket.broadcast.to(channel).emit('Bye');

        // Close socket from server's side
        socket.disconnect();
    });

    // Handle 'Ack' messages
    socket.on('Ack', function () {
        console.log('Got an Ack!');
        // Close socket from server's side
        socket.disconnect();
    });

    // Utility function used for remote logging
    function log(){
        var array = [">>> "];
        for (var i = 0; i < arguments.length; i++) {
                array.push(arguments[i]);
        }
        socket.emit('log', array);
    }
});
```

We're now ready to get started with our signaling example walk-through.

Creating the Signaling Channel

We herein focus on the very first steps of the example call flow, as illustrated in Figure 4-2.

Let's assume that a first client using the Chrome browser loads the HTML5 page of Example 4-1. The page first connects to the server and then prompts the user for the name of the channel (Figure 4-3):

```
...
// Connect to server
var socket = io.connect('http://localhost:8181');

// Ask channel name from user
channel = prompt("Enter signaling channel name:");
...
```

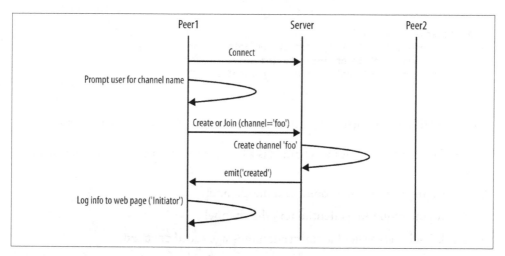

Figure 4-2. The first steps: Channel creation

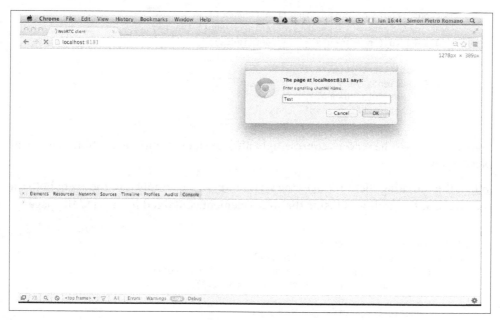

Figure 4-3. The example page loaded in Chrome (channel initiator)

Once the user fills in the channel name field and hits the OK button, the JavaScript code in the page sends a `create` or `join` message to the server:

```
...
if (channel !== "") {
    console.log('Trying to create or join channel: ', channel);
    // Send 'create or join' to the server
    socket.emit('create or join', channel);
}
...
```

Upon reception of the client's request, the server performs the following actions:

1. Verifies that the mentioned channel is a brand new one (i.e., there are no clients in it)

2. Associates a server-side room with the channel

3. Allows the requesting client to join the channel

4. Sends back to the client a notification message called `created`

The following snippet shows this sequence of actions:

```
...
socket.on('create or join', function (channel) {
    var numClients = io.sockets.clients(channel).length;
    console.log('numclients = ' + numClients);

    // First client joining...
    if (numClients == 0){
        socket.join(channel);
        socket.emit('created', channel);
...
```

Figure 4-4 shows the server's console right after the aforementioned actions have been performed.

When the initiating client receives the server's answer, it simply logs the event both on the JavaScript console and inside the <div> element contained in the HTML5 page:

```
...
// Handle 'created' message
socket.on('created', function (channel){
    console.log('channel ' + channel + ' has been created!');
    console.log('This peer is the initiator...');

    // Dynamically modify the HTML5 page
    div.insertAdjacentHTML( 'beforeEnd', '<p>Time: ' +
        (performance.now() / 1000).toFixed(3) + ' --> Channel ' +
        channel + ' has been created! </p>');

    div.insertAdjacentHTML( 'beforeEnd', '<p>Time: ' +
        (performance.now() / 1000).toFixed(3) +
        ' --> This peer is the initiator...</p>');
});
...
```

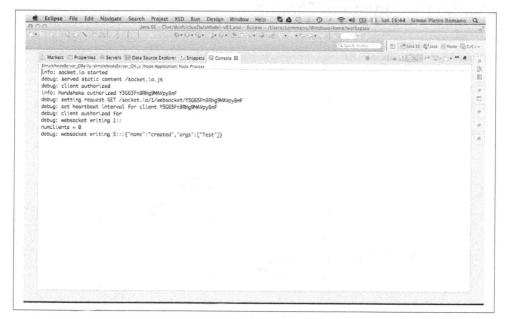

Figure 4-4. Signaling server managing initiator's request

The situation described above is illustrated in Figure 4-5.

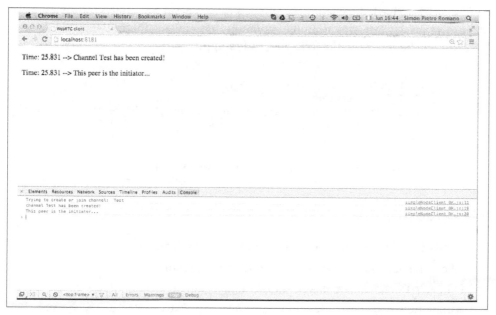

Figure 4-5. Initiator's window after channel creation

Joining the Signaling Channel

Let's now move on to the second client, the *channel joiner*, focusing on the call flow section shown in Figure 4-6.

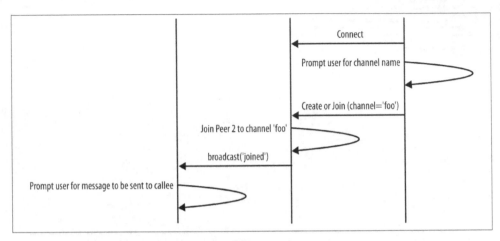

Figure 4-6. Joining an already existing channel

For the sake of completeness, we will this time use Firefox as the client browser, the look and feel of which, right after loading the application page, is illustrated in Figure 4-7.

As already described, the client first connects to the server and then sends it a `create` or `join` request. Since this time the requesting peer is not the initiator, the server's behavior will be driven by the following code snippet:

```
...
    } else if (numClients == 1) {
        // Inform initiator...
        io.sockets.in(channel).emit('remotePeerJoining', channel);
            // Let the new peer join channel
        socket.join(channel);

        socket.broadcast.to(channel).emit('broadcast: joined', 'S -->
            broadcast(): client ' + socket.id + ' joined channel ' + channel);
...
```

Basically, the server will:

1. Notify the channel initiator of the arrival of a new `join` request.

2. Allow the new client to enter the already existing room.

3. Update (through a `broadcast` message) the channel initiator about the successful completion of the `join` operation, allowing it to prepare to start a new conversation.

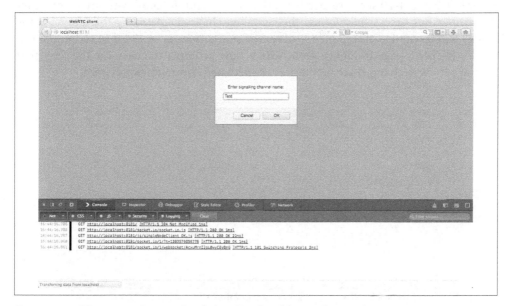

Figure 4-7. The example page loaded in Firefox (channel joiner)

Such a sequence of actions is reported in Figure 4-8, which shows the server's console at this stage of the call flow.

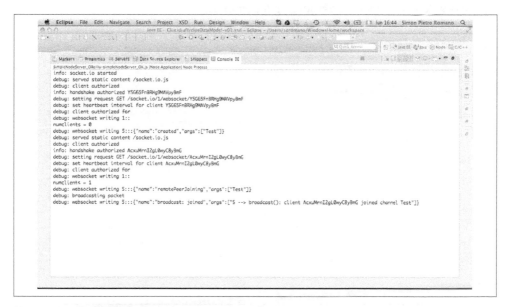

Figure 4-8. Signaling server managing joiner's request

Figures 4-9 and 4-10 show, respectively, the joiner's and initiator's windows right after the former has successfully joined the signaling channel created by the latter. As the reader will recognize, this sequence of server-side actions is reported in red in the initiator's HTML5 page in Figure 4-10, which now prompts the user for the very first message to be exchanged across the server-mediated communication path.

Figure 4-9. Joiner's window after joining the channel

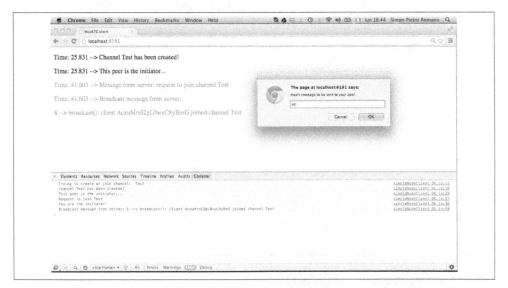

Figure 4-10. Starting a conversation after channel setup

Starting a Server-Mediated Conversation

We have now arrived at the call flow stage reported in Figure 4-11, which basically captures the core of the application. In this phase, in fact, the initiator sends a first message to the joiner, who is first notified of this event and then prompted for the introduction of a proper answer.

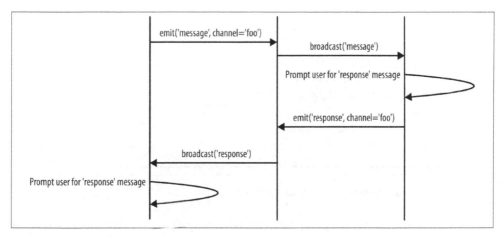

Figure 4-11. Starting a conversation

As usual, the client retrieves the user's input and emits a message towards the server in order for it to be properly dispatched. On the server's side, the received message is simply broadcast[1] on the channel:

```
...
    // Handle 'message' messages
    socket.on('message', function (message) {
        log('S --> Got message: ', message);

        socket.broadcast.to(message.channel).emit('message', message.message);
    });
...
```

The above described server's behavior is illustrated in the console snapshot of Figure 4-12.

---

1. Note that broadcasting on a channel made of just two peers is equivalent to sending a notification to the peer who was not the sender of the message itself.

Figure 4-12. Signaling server acting as a relay node

Figure 4-13 shows the remote peer (the joiner) that has just received the message relayed by the server.

Figure 4-13. Remote peer receiving relayed message from signaling server

As evidenced by the figure, the following actions are performed:

1. Logging the received message both on the JavaScript console and on the HTML5 page
2. Prompting the receiver for proper input
3. Sending the receiver's answer back to the sender (across the signaling channel)

Such a sequence is driven by the following code snippet:

```
...
// Handle 'message' message
socket.on('message', function (message){
  console.log('Got message from other peer: ' + message);

  div.insertAdjacentHTML( 'beforeEnd', '<p>Time: ' +
    (performance.now() / 1000).toFixed(3) +
    ' --> Got message from other peer: </p>');

  div.insertAdjacentHTML( 'beforeEnd', '<p style="color:blue">' +
    message + '</p>');

  // Send back response message:
  // 1. Get response from user
  var myResponse = prompt('Send response to other peer:', "");

  // 2. Send it to remote peer (through server)
  socket.emit('response', {
    channel: channel,
        message: myResponse});

});
...
```

As soon as the receiver hits the OK button on the prompt window in Figure 4-14, the response message is emitted towards the server, which forwards it to the remote party:

```
...
// Handle 'response' messages
socket.on('response', function (response) {
    log('S --> Got response: ', response);

    // Just forward message to the other peer
    socket.broadcast.to(response.channel).emit('response',
        response.message);
});
...
```

This behavior is once again illustrated by the server's console snapshot in Figure 4-14.

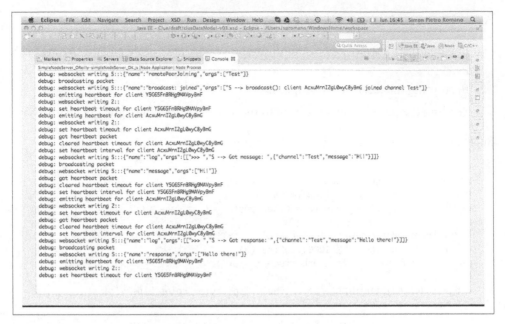

Figure 4-14. Signaling server relaying remote peer's response

Continuing to Chat Across the Channel

We are now in the steady-state portion of the application (Figure 4-15), where the two peers simply take turns in asking the server to relay messages towards the other party.

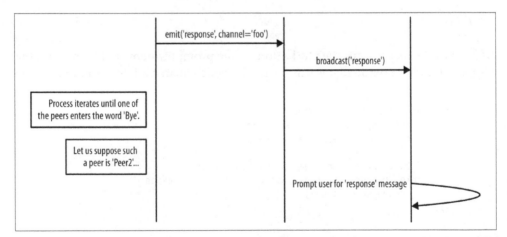

Figure 4-15. Signaling channel use in the steady state

Message exchanging is achieved on the client's side through the following code:

```
...
// Handle 'response' message
socket.on('response', function (response){
  console.log('Got response from other peer: ' + response);

  div.insertAdjacentHTML( 'beforeEnd', '<p>Time: ' +
    (performance.now() / 1000).toFixed(3) +
    ' --> Got response from other peer: </p>');

  div.insertAdjacentHTML( 'beforeEnd', '<p style="color:blue">' +
    response + '</p>');

  // Keep on chatting
  var chatMessage = prompt('Keep on chatting. Write \
                           "Bye" to quit conversation', "");
  ...
  ...
    // Keep on going: send response back to remote party (through server)
  socket.emit('response', {
    channel: channel,
    message: chatMessage});
  }
});
```

Basically, upon reception of a new message, each peer performs the usual logging operations and then prompts the user for new input. As long as the inserted text has a value other than *Bye*, it sends a new message to the remote party. Figure 4-16 shows the initiator's window right before a new message is emitted across the channel.

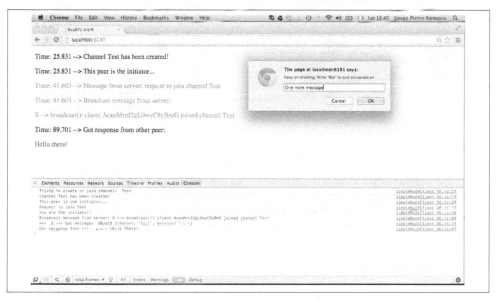

Figure 4-16. Continuing the chat (initiator's side)

Figure 4-17 in turn shows the server's console upon reception of such a message, which is, as usual, broadcast to the remote party.

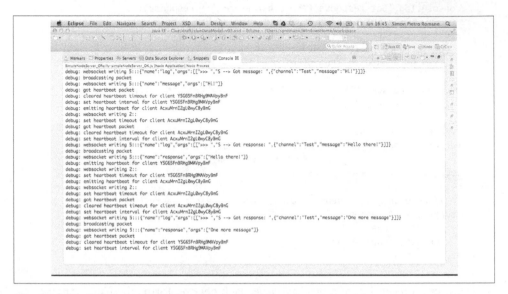

Figure 4-17. Continuing the chat (server's side)

Finally, Figure 4-18 shows reception of the relayed message on the receiver's side.

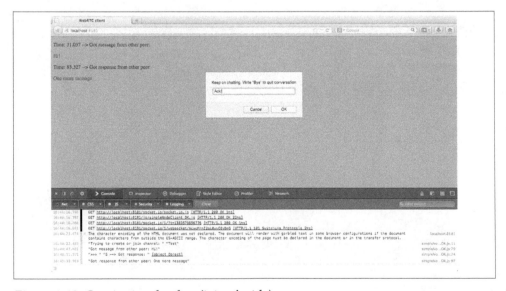

Figure 4-18. Continuing the chat (joiner's side)

Closing the Signaling Channel

We are now ready to analyze channel teardown, as described in the call flow snippet in Figure 4-19.

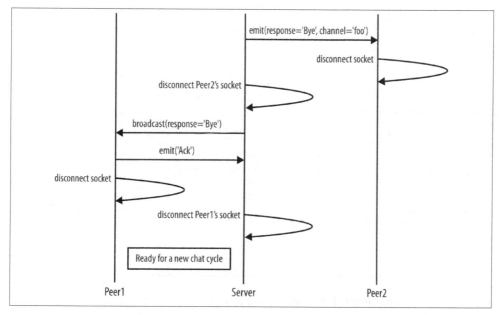

Figure 4-19. Closing the signaling channel

The teardown procedure is actually triggered by the insertion of a *Bye* message in one of the two browsers (see Figure 4-20).

What happens behind the scenes is the following:

```
...
// User wants to quit conversation: send 'Bye' to remote party
if(chatMessage == "Bye"){
  div.insertAdjacentHTML( 'beforeEnd', '<p>Time: ' +
      (performance.now() / 1000).toFixed(3) +
      ' --> Sending "Bye" to server...</p>');
  console.log('Sending "Bye" to server');

  socket.emit('Bye', channel);

  div.insertAdjacentHTML( 'beforeEnd', '<p>Time: ' +
      (performance.now() / 1000).toFixed(3) +
      ' --> Going to disconnect...</p>');
  console.log('Going to disconnect...');

  // Disconnect from server
```

```
    socket.disconnect();
    }
...
```

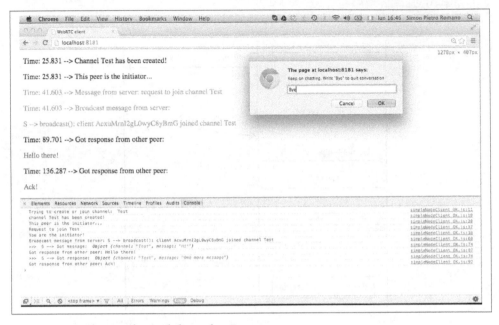

Figure 4-20. Closing channel through a Bye message

As we can see in the code, the disconnecting client first sends a *Bye* message across the channel and immediately thereafter closes the web socket (Figure 4-21).

As soon as the server gets the *Bye* message, it first relays it to the remote party and then closes the communication channel towards the disconnecting client:

```
...
    // Handle 'Bye' messages
    socket.on('Bye', function(channel){
        // Notify other peer
        socket.broadcast.to(channel).emit('Bye');

        // Close socket from server's side
        socket.disconnect();
    });

...
```

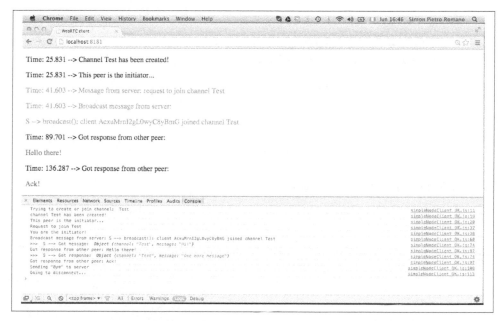

Figure 4-21. Initiator's disconnection

Let's finally analyze the behavior of the peer receiving the *Bye* message from the remote party. The peer first logs information about the received message (both on the JavaScript console and inside the HTML5 page):

```
...
// Handle 'Bye' message
socket.on('Bye', function (){
  console.log('Got "Bye" from other peer! Going to disconnect...');

  div.insertAdjacentHTML( 'beforeEnd', '<p>Time: ' +
    (performance.now() / 1000).toFixed(3) +
    ' --> Got "Bye" from other peer!</p>');
...
```

Then, an *Ack* message is sent back to the server to confirm reception of the disconnection request:

```
...
  div.insertAdjacentHTML( 'beforeEnd', '<p>Time: ' +
    (performance.now() / 1000).toFixed(3) +
    ' --> Sending "Ack" to server</p>');

  // Send 'Ack' back to remote party (through server)
  console.log('Sending "Ack" to server');

  socket.emit('Ack');
```

```
// Disconnect from server
div.insertAdjacentHTML( 'beforeEnd', '<p>Time: ' +
  (performance.now() / 1000).toFixed(3) +
  ' --> Going to disconnect...</p>');

console.log('Going to disconnect...');

socket.disconnect();
...
```

Finally, the receiving peer tears down its own connection to the server:

```
...
console.log('Going to disconnect...');

socket.disconnect();
});
```

The above sequence of actions can be easily identified in the snapshot in Figure 4-22.

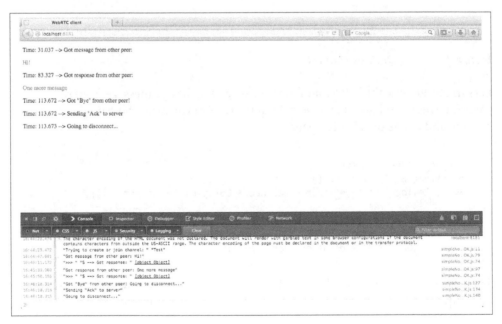

Figure 4-22. Remote peer handling relayed disconnection message and disconnecting

The final actions are undertaken on the server's side. Reception of the *Ack* message is logged on the console (see Figure 4-23) and the channel is eventually torn down:

```
// Handle 'Ack' messages
socket.on('Ack', function () {
    console.log('Got an Ack!');
    // Close socket from server's side
    socket.disconnect();
});
```

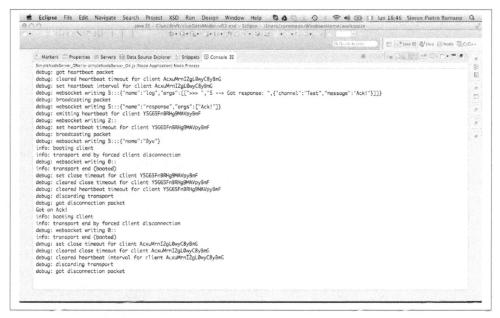

Figure 4-23. Closing channel on the server's side

CHAPTER 5

Putting It All Together: Your First WebRTC System from Scratch

We are finally ready to put all the pieces together and build our first WebRTC application. In this chapter, by leveraging a signaling server like the one we described in Chapter 4, we will implement the Browser RTC Trapezoid in a distributed scenario. Basically, we will take the running example of Chapter 3 and let it also work beyond the limits of a local perspective.

We will show how to use the signaling channel to allow two peers to exchange user media information, session descriptions, and ICE protocol candidates. We will also highlight how the signaling server role proves fundamental only during the setup phase. Indeed, once the above information has been successfully exchanged, the communication paradigm switches to pure peer-to-peer, with the server itself having no involvement in the actual data exchange phases.

A Complete WebRTC Call Flow

Figures 5-1, 5-2, and 5-3 provide the big picture associated with a complete WebRTC call flow involving a channel *Initiator*, a channel *Joiner*, and a signaling server relaying messages between them at channel setup time.

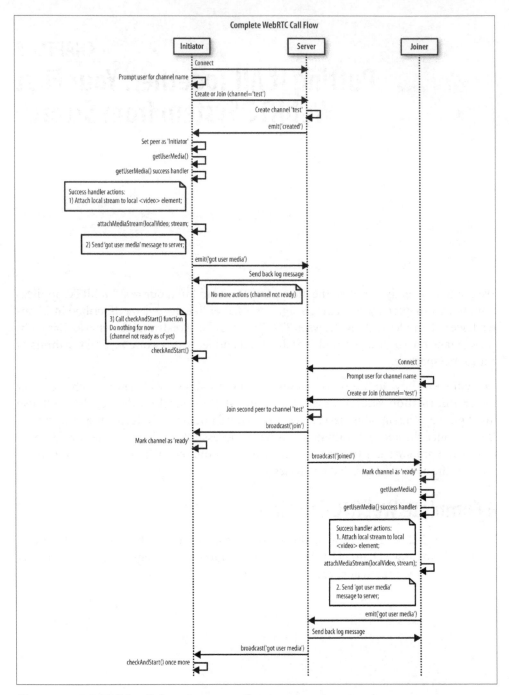

Figure 5-1. WebRTC call flow: Sequence diagram, part 1

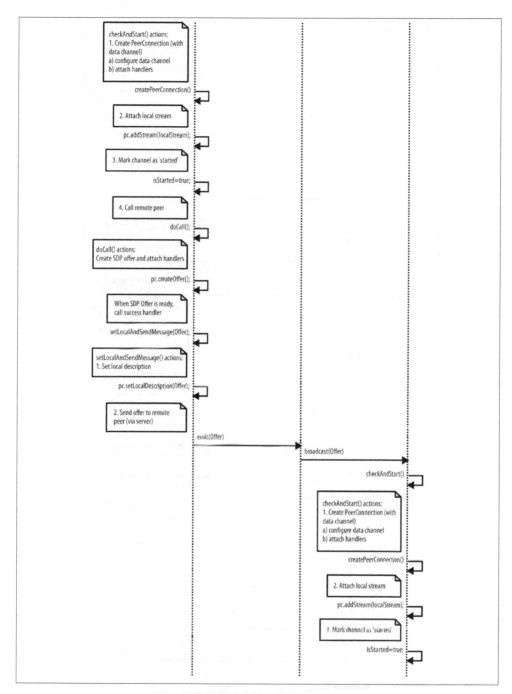

Figure 5-2. WebRTC call flow: Sequence diagram, part 2

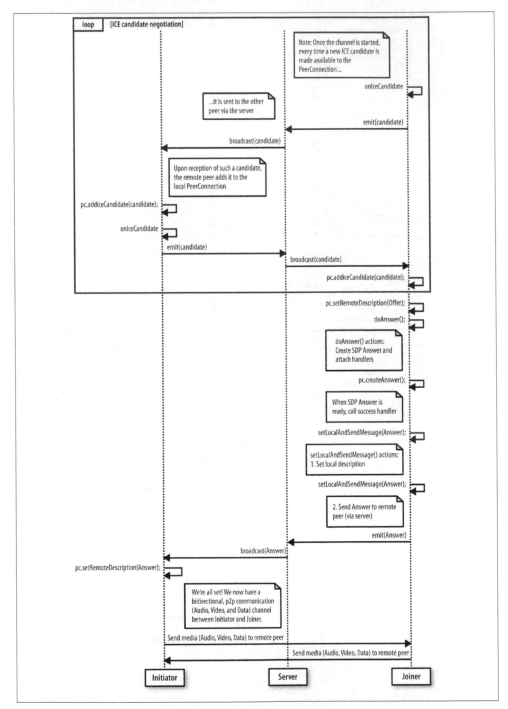

Figure 5-3. WebRTC call flow: Sequence diagram, part 3

The sequence diagram evolves through the following macrosteps:

1. The Initiator connects to the server and lets it create the signaling channel.
2. The Initiator (after getting the user's consent) gets access to the user's media.
3. The Joiner connects to the server and joins the channel.
4. When the Joiner also gets access to the local user's media, a message is sent to the Initiator (through the server), triggering the negotiation procedure:

   - The Initiator creates a `PeerConnection`, adds the local stream to it, creates an SDP offer, and sends it to the Joiner via the signaling server.
   - Upon receipt of the SDP offer, the Joiner mirrors the behavior of the Initiator by creating a `PeerConnection` object, adding the local stream to it, and building an SDP answer to be sent back (via the server) to the remote party.

5. During negotiation, the two parties leverage the signaling server to exchange network reachability information (in the form of ICE protocol candidate addresses).
6. When the Initiator receives the Joiner's answer to its own offer, the negotiation procedure is over: the two parties switch to peer-to-peer communication by exploiting their respective `PeerConnection` objects, which have also been equipped with a data channel that can be used to exchange text messages directly.

In the following sections, we will walk through these steps by analyzing each of them in further detail. Before doing so, let us introduce the simple web application we devised as a running example for this chapter; the HTML code is reported in Example 5-1.

Example 5-1. Simple WebRTC application

```
<!DOCTYPE html>
<html>
<head>

<title>Very simple WebRTC application with a Node.js signaling server</title>

</head>

<body>

<div id='mainDiv'>

    <table border="1" width="100%">
            <tr>
                <th>
                        Local video
                </th>
                <th>
                        Remote video
```

```
                </th>
        </tr>
        <tr>
                <td>
                        <video id="localVideo" autoplay></video>
                </td>
                <td>
                        <video id="remoteVideo" autoplay></video>
                </td>
        </tr>
        <tr>
                <td align="center">
                        <textarea rows="4" cols="60"
        id="dataChannelSend" disabled
                        placeholder="This will be enabled once
        the data channel is up...">
        </textarea>
                </td>
                <td align="center">
                        <textarea rows="4" cols="60"
        id="dataChannelReceive" disabled>
        </textarea>
                </td>
        </tr>
        <tr>
                <td align="center">
                        <button id="sendButton" disabled>Send</button>
                </td>
                <td></td>
        </tr>
        </table>
</div>

<script src='/socket.io/socket.io.js'></script>
<script src='js/lib/adapter.js'></script>
<script src='js/completeNodeClientWithDataChannel.js'></script>

</body>
</html>
```

Local video, as well as local data channel information, are shown on the left side of the page, whereas remote video and data are reproduced on the right side of the window. The page refers to three script files, the first of which is the already introduced `sock et.io` library (see "The socket.io JavaScript Library" on page 66). As to the second file (*adapter.js*), it is a handy JavaScript *shim* library that helps the programmer by properly abstracting browser prefixes, as well as other browser differences and changes in the way vendors are currently interpreting the specs. Finally, *completeNodeClientWithDataChannel.js* contains the actual client code and is presented in Example 5-2 in its entirety for the benefit of the reader. We will dig into the details of this file in the remainder of this chapter.

Example 5-2. completeNodeClientWithDataChannel.js

```javascript
'use strict';

// Look after different browser vendors' ways of calling the getUserMedia()
// API method:
// Opera --> getUserMedia
// Chrome --> webkitGetUserMedia
// Firefox --> mozGetUserMedia
navigator.getUserMedia = navigator.getUserMedia ||
    navigator.webkitGetUserMedia || navigator.mozGetUserMedia;

// Clean-up function:
// collect garbage before unloading browser's window
window.onbeforeunload = function(e){
        hangup();
}

// Data channel information
var sendChannel, receiveChannel;
var sendButton = document.getElementById("sendButton");
var sendTextarea = document.getElementById("dataChannelSend");
var receiveTextarea = document.getElementById("dataChannelReceive");

// HTML5 <video> elements
var localVideo = document.querySelector('#localVideo');
var remoteVideo = document.querySelector('#remoteVideo');

// Handler associated with Send button
sendButton.onclick = sendData;

// Flags...
var isChannelReady = false;
var isInitiator = false;
var isStarted = false;

// WebRTC data structures
// Streams
var localStream;
var remoteStream;
// PeerConnection
var pc;

// PeerConnection ICE protocol configuration (either Firefox or Chrome)
var pc_config = webrtcDetectedBrowser === 'firefox' ?
  {'iceServers':[{'url':'stun:23.21.150.121'}]} : // IP address
  {'iceServers': [{'url': 'stun:stun.l.google.com:19302'}]};

var pc_constraints = {
  'optional': [
    {'DtlsSrtpKeyAgreement': true}
  ]};
```

```
var sdpConstraints = {};

// Let's get started: prompt user for input (room name)
var room = prompt('Enter room name:');

// Connect to signaling server
var socket = io.connect("http://localhost:8181");

// Send 'Create or join' message to singnaling server
if (room !== '') {
  console.log('Create or join room', room);
  socket.emit('create or join', room);
}

// Set getUserMedia constraints
var constraints = {video: true, audio: true};

// From this point on, execution proceeds based on asynchronous events...

// getUserMedia() handlers...

function handleUserMedia(stream) {
        localStream = stream;
        attachMediaStream(localVideo, stream);
        console.log('Adding local stream.');
        sendMessage('got user media');
}

function handleUserMediaError(error){
        console.log('navigator.getUserMedia error: ', error);
}

// Server-mediated message exchanging...

// 1. Server-->Client...

// Handle 'created' message coming back from server:
// this peer is the initiator
socket.on('created', function (room){
  console.log('Created room ' + room);
  isInitiator = true;

  // Call getUserMedia()
  navigator.getUserMedia(constraints, handleUserMedia, handleUserMediaError);
  console.log('Getting user media with constraints', constraints);

  checkAndStart();
});

// Handle 'full' message coming back from server:
// this peer arrived too late :-(
```

```javascript
socket.on('full', function (room){
  console.log('Room ' + room + ' is full');
});

// Handle 'join' message coming back from server:
// another peer is joining the channel
socket.on('join', function (room){
  console.log('Another peer made a request to join room ' + room);
  console.log('This peer is the initiator of room ' + room + '!');
  isChannelReady = true;
});

// Handle 'joined' message coming back from server:
// this is the second peer joining the channel
socket.on('joined', function (room){
  console.log('This peer has joined room ' + room);
  isChannelReady = true;

  // Call getUserMedia()
  navigator.getUserMedia(constraints, handleUserMedia, handleUserMediaError);
  console.log('Getting user media with constraints', constraints);
});

// Server-sent log message...
socket.on('log', function (array){
  console.log.apply(console, array);
});

// Receive message from the other peer via the signaling server
socket.on('message', function (message){
  console.log('Received message:', message);
  if (message === 'got user media') {
      checkAndStart();
  } else if (message.type === 'offer') {
    if (!isInitiator && !isStarted) {
      checkAndStart();
    }
    pc.setRemoteDescription(new RTCSessionDescription(message));
    doAnswer();
  } else if (message.type === 'answer' && isStarted) {
    pc.setRemoteDescription(new RTCSessionDescription(message));
  } else if (message.type === 'candidate' && isStarted) {
    var candidate = new RTCIceCandidate({sdpMLineIndex:message.label,
      candidate:message.candidate});
    pc.addIceCandidate(candidate);
  } else if (message === 'bye' && isStarted) {
    handleRemoteHangup();
  }
});

// 2. Client-->Server
```

```
// Send message to the other peer via the signaling server
function sendMessage(message){
  console.log('Sending message: ', message);
  socket.emit('message', message);
}

// Channel negotiation trigger function
function checkAndStart() {

  if (!isStarted && typeof localStream != 'undefined' && isChannelReady) {
        createPeerConnection();
    isStarted = true;
    if (isInitiator) {
      doCall();
    }
  }
}

// PeerConnection management...
function createPeerConnection() {
  try {
    pc = new RTCPeerConnection(pc_config, pc_constraints);

    pc.addStream(localStream);

    pc.onicecandidate = handleIceCandidate;
    console.log('Created RTCPeerConnnection with:\n' +
        ' config: \'' + JSON.stringify(pc_config) + '\';\n' +
        ' constraints: \'' + JSON.stringify(pc_constraints) + '\'.');
  } catch (e) {
    console.log('Failed to create PeerConnection, exception: ' + e.message);
    alert('Cannot create RTCPeerConnection object.');
      return;
  }

  pc.onaddstream = handleRemoteStreamAdded;
  pc.onremovestream = handleRemoteStreamRemoved;

  if (isInitiator) {
    try {
      // Create a reliable data channel
      sendChannel = pc.createDataChannel("sendDataChannel",
        {reliable: true});
      trace('Created send data channel');
    } catch (e) {
      alert('Failed to create data channel. ');
      trace('createDataChannel() failed with exception: ' + e.message);
    }
    sendChannel.onopen = handleSendChannelStateChange;
    sendChannel.onmessage = handleMessage;
    sendChannel.onclose = handleSendChannelStateChange;
  } else { // Joiner
```

```
      pc.ondatachannel = gotReceiveChannel;
  }
}

// Data channel management
function sendData() {
  var data = sendTextarea.value;
  if(isInitiator) sendChannel.send(data);
  else receiveChannel.send(data);
  trace('Sent data: ' + data);
}

// Handlers...

function gotReceiveChannel(event) {
  trace('Receive Channel Callback');
  receiveChannel = event.channel;
  receiveChannel.onmessage = handleMessage;
  receiveChannel.onopen = handleReceiveChannelStateChange;
  receiveChannel.onclose = handleReceiveChannelStateChange;
}

function handleMessage(event) {
  trace('Received message: ' + event.data);
  receiveTextarea.value += event.data + '\n';
}

function handleSendChannelStateChange() {
  var readyState = sendChannel.readyState;
  trace('Send channel state is: ' + readyState);
  // If channel ready, enable user's input
  if (readyState == "open") {
    dataChannelSend.disabled = false;
    dataChannelSend.focus();
    dataChannelSend.placeholder = "";
    sendButton.disabled = false;
  } else {
    dataChannelSend.disabled = true;
    sendButton.disabled = true;
  }
}

function handleReceiveChannelStateChange() {
  var readyState = receiveChannel.readyState;
  trace('Receive channel state is: ' + readyState);
  // If channel ready, enable user's input
  if (readyState == "open") {
          dataChannelSend.disabled = false;
          dataChannelSend.focus();
          dataChannelSend.placeholder = "";
          sendButton.disabled = false;
        } else {
```

```
        dataChannelSend.disabled = true;
        sendButton.disabled = true;
    }
}

// ICE candidates management
function handleIceCandidate(event) {
  console.log('handleIceCandidate event: ', event);
  if (event.candidate) {
    sendMessage({
      type: 'candidate',
      label: event.candidate.sdpMLineIndex,
      id: event.candidate.sdpMid,
      candidate: event.candidate.candidate});
  } else {
    console.log('End of candidates.');
  }
}

// Create Offer
function doCall() {
  console.log('Creating Offer...');
  pc.createOffer(setLocalAndSendMessage, onSignalingError, sdpConstraints);
}

// Signaling error handler
function onSignalingError(error) {
        console.log('Failed to create signaling message : ' + error.name);
}

// Create Answer
function doAnswer() {
  console.log('Sending answer to peer.');
  pc.createAnswer(setLocalAndSendMessage, onSignalingError, sdpConstraints);
}

// Success handler for both createOffer()
// and createAnswer()
function setLocalAndSendMessage(sessionDescription) {
  pc.setLocalDescription(sessionDescription);
  sendMessage(sessionDescription);
}

// Remote stream handlers...

function handleRemoteStreamAdded(event) {
  console.log('Remote stream added.');
  attachMediaStream(remoteVideo, event.stream);
  console.log('Remote stream attached!!.');
  remoteStream = event.stream;
}
```

```
function handleRemoteStreamRemoved(event) {
  console.log('Remote stream removed. Event: ', event);
}

// Clean-up functions...

function hangup() {
  console.log('Hanging up.');
  stop();
  sendMessage('bye');
}

function handleRemoteHangup() {
  console.log('Session terminated.');
  stop();
  isInitiator = false;
}

function stop() {
  isStarted = false;
  if (sendChannel) sendChannel.close();
  if (receiveChannel) receiveChannel.close();
  if (pc) pc.close();
  pc = null;
  sendButton.disabled=true;
}
```

Based on the information contained in Chapter 4, the reader should face no issues in understanding the behavior of the signaling server, which has been written as a Node.js application and whose code is reproduced in the following:

```
var static = require('node-static');
var http = require('http');
// Create a node-static server instance
var file = new(static.Server)();

// We use the http module's createServer function and
// rely on our instance of node-static to serve the files
var app = http.createServer(function (req, res) {
  file.serve(req, res);
}).listen(8181);

// Use socket.io JavaScript library for real-time web applications
var io = require('socket.io').listen(app);

// let's start managing connections...
io.sockets.on('connection', function (socket){

      // Handle 'message' messages
    socket.on('message', function (message) {
        log('S --> got message: ', message);
        // channel-only broadcast...
```

```
            socket.broadcast.to(message.channel).emit('message', message);
        });

        // Handle 'create or join' messages
        socket.on('create or join', function (room) {
            var numClients = io.sockets.clients(room).length;

            log('S --> Room ' + room + ' has ' + numClients + ' client(s)');
            log('S --> Request to create or join room', room);

            // First client joining...
            if (numClients == 0){
                socket.join(room);
                socket.emit('created', room);
            } else if (numClients == 1) {
            // Second client joining...
                io.sockets.in(room).emit('join', room);
                socket.join(room);
                socket.emit('joined', room);
            } else { // max two clients
                socket.emit('full', room);
            }
        });

        function log(){
            var array = [">>> "];
            for (var i = 0; i < arguments.length; i++) {
                    array.push(arguments[i]);
            }
            socket.emit('log', array);
        }
    });
```

Basically, the server looks after both channel management operations (*creation* upon reception of the Initiator's request, *join* when the second peer arrives) and message relaying (at session setup time). As already anticipated, it completes its tasks right after a peer-to-peer session between the two browsers sharing the signaling channel has been successfully instantiated.

Let's now get started with our complete WebRTC example walk-through.

Initiator Joining the Channel

Figure 5-4 shows the sequence of actions undertaken by the Initiator when the sample WebRTC application described in the previous section is started.

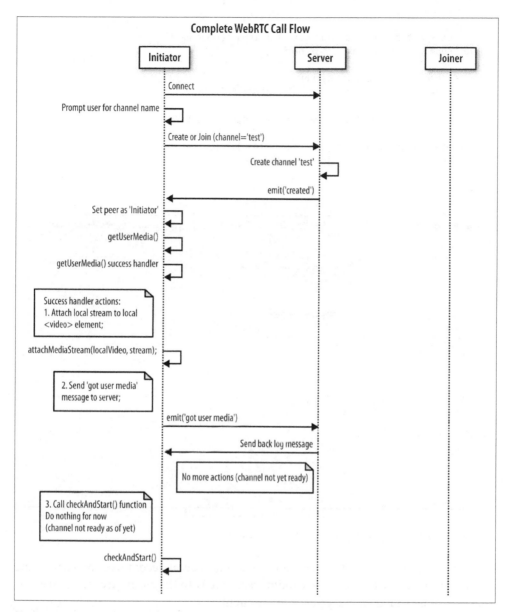

Figure 5-4. Initiator joining the channel

As shown in the figure, as soon as the web page is loaded in the browser, the user is first prompted for the channel name; then, the peer connects to the signaling server and sends it a `create` or `join` message. This is reported in the JavaScript snippet below and also shown in the snapshot in Figure 5-5:

```
...
// Let's get started: prompt user for input (room name)
var room = prompt('Enter room name:');

// Connect to signalling server
var socket = io.connect("http://localhost:8181");

// Send 'create' or 'join' message to singnalling server
if (room !== '') {
  console.log('Create or join room', room);
  socket.emit('create or join', room);
}
...
```

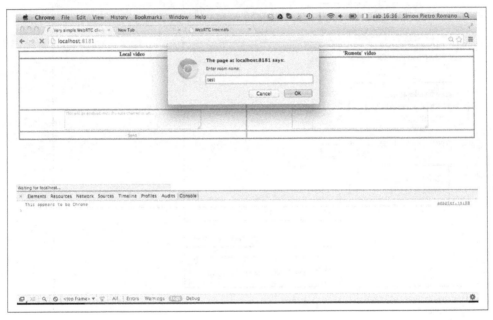

Figure 5-5. Initiator joining with Chrome browser

When the server receives the `create` or `join` message, it recognizes the peer as the Initiator and creates the server-side room associated with the required channel. It eventually sends a `created` message back to the client:

```
...
// Handle 'create or join' messages
    socket.on('create or join', function (room) {
        var numClients = io.sockets.clients(room).length;

        log('S --> Room ' + room + ' has ' + numClients + ' client(s)');
        log('S --> Request to create or join room', room);
```

```
// First client joining...
if (numClients == 0){
    socket.join(room);
    socket.emit('created', room);
} else if (numClients == 1) {
    ...
...
```

Figure 5-6 shows the server's console at this stage.

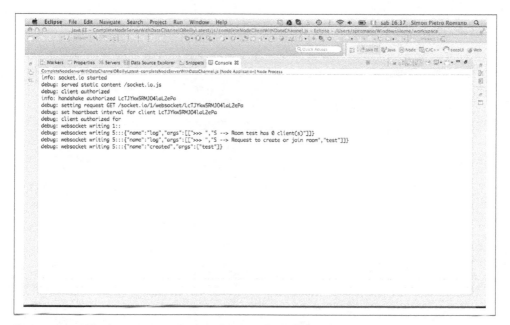

Figure 5-6. Signaling server creating the signaling channel

We have now reached the point where the client gets a `created` message back from the server and realizes it is going to play the role of the channel initiator:

```
// Handle 'created' message coming back from server:
// this peer is the initiator
socket.on('created', function (room){
  console.log('Created room ' + room);
  isInitiator = true;
  ...
```

The next action undertaken by the client is getting access to the user's media through the `getUserMedia()` API call:

```
...
    // Call getUserMedia()
    navigator.getUserMedia(constraints, handleUserMedia, handleUserMediaError);
    console.log('Getting user media with constraints', constraints);
    ...
```

Figure 5-7 shows the browser's window right before getting the user's consent.

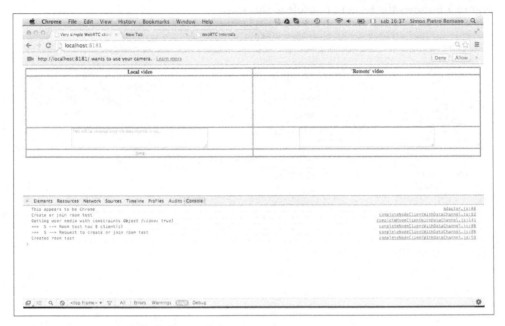

Figure 5-7. Initiator asking for user's consent

The following snapshot reports the actions performed by the handleUserMedia() success handler: (1) the retrieved video stream is attached to the local <video> element of
the HTML page; and (2) a got user media message is sent to the server.

```
...
function handleUserMedia(stream) {
    localStream = stream;
        attachMediaStream(localVideo, stream);
        console.log('Adding local stream.');
        sendMessage('got user media');
}
...
```

The effect of the first of these actions is shown in Figure 5-8.

Figure 5-8. Initiator after user's consent

The JavaScript code used to send messages to the server is given below:

```
...
// Send message to the other peer via the signaling server
function sendMessage(message){
  console.log('Sending message: ', message);
  socket.emit('message', message);
}
...
```

Server-side behavior associated with the reception of a generic message is shown in the following excerpt. The server first sends a logging message (which is also visible in the browser's console in the lower part of Figure 5-8) back to the client and then broadcasts the received message to the remote party, if it exists (which is not the case at this point of the call flow):

```
...
// Handle 'message' messages
    socket.on('message', function (message) {
        log('S --> got message: ', message);
        // channel only broadcast...
        socket.broadcast.to(message.channel).emit('message', message);
    });
...
```

The last action performed by the channel initiator is the execution of the `checkAnd` `Start()` function, which, at this stage of the overall call flow, actually does nothing, since the channel is not yet ready:

```
...
function checkAndStart() {
  // Do nothing if channel not ready...
  if (!isStarted && typeof localStream != 'undefined' && isChannelReady) {
    ...
  ...
```

Joiner Joining the Channel

Let's now figure out what happens when the second peer joins the channel. The relevant sequence of actions is illustrated in Figure 5-9.

The first part of the diagram mirrors the behavior of the Initiator, prompting the user for a channel name and sending a `create` or `join` message to the server. Message handling on the server's side (with the server's console reported in Figure 5-10) this time envisages that a `join` message is sent to the Initiator (who can now mark the channel as *ready*), immediately followed by a `joined` response towards the Joiner:

```
...
    } else if (numClients == 1) {
    // Second client joining...
        io.sockets.in(room).emit('join', room);
        socket.join(room);
        socket.emit('joined', room);
    } else { // max two clients
    ...
```

The following excerpt shows the client-side actions associated with the reception of a `join` message:

```
...
// Handle 'join' message coming back from server:
// another peer is joining the channel
socket.on('join', function (room){
  console.log('Another peer made a request to join room ' + room);
  console.log('This peer is the initiator of room ' + room + '!');
  isChannelReady = true;
});
...
```

Finally, the following JavaScript illustrates how the client realizes that it is playing the Joiner's role since it gets back a `joined` response to the `create` or `join` request:

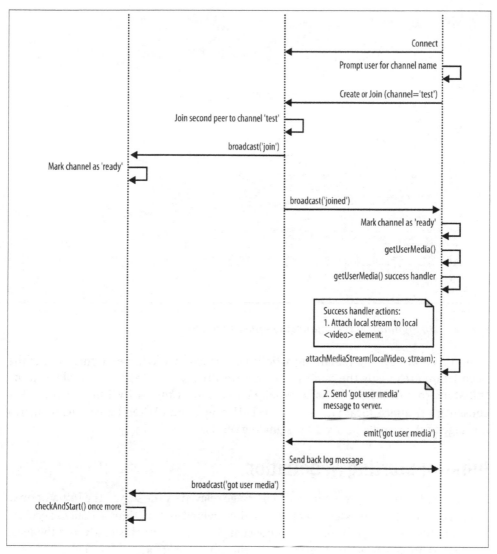

Figure 5-9. Joiner joining the channel

```
...
// Handle 'joined' message coming back from server:
// this is the second peer joining the channel
socket.on('joined', function (room){
  console.log('This peer has joined room ' + room);
  isChannelReady = true;
});
...
```

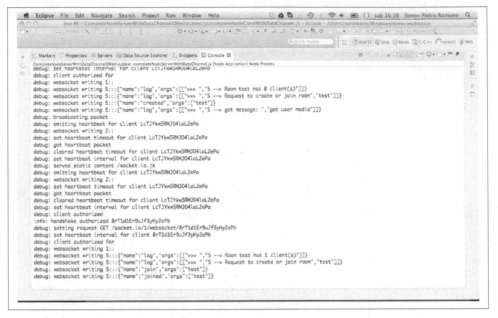

Figure 5-10. Signaling server managing Joiner's request

From this point on, the remaining actions performed by the Joiner at this stage of the negotiation are exactly the same as the ones we already described when looking at the Initiator's role in the previous section: (1) access local media (waiting for the user's consent); (2) attach local video to the HTML page; and (3) send a got user media message to the remote peer via the signaling server.

Initiator Starting Negotiation

Upon reception of the got user media message relayed by the server, the Initiator once again activates the checkAndStart() function, which is this time actually executed, since the boundary conditions have now changed: the channel is ready and the local stream has already been made available by the getUserMedia() API call.

The UML snapshot in Figure 5-11 and the following JavaScript code indicate that the Initiator (1) creates a PeerConnection object; (2) marks the channel as *started*; and (3) activates the doCall() JavaScript function.

```
...
// Channel negotiation trigger function
function checkAndStart() {
  if (!isStarted && typeof localStream != 'undefined' && isChannelReady) {
    createPeerConnection();
    isStarted = true;
```

```
    if (isInitiator) {
      doCall();
    }
  }
}
...
```

Digging into the details of the above actions, the following code excerpt shows that a number of handlers are attached to the PeerConnection object in order to properly manage both ICE candidate addresses and remote stream addition and removal. Furthermore, the PeerConnection is also equipped with a data channel that will be used to exchange text data with the Joiner, in a peer-to-peer fashion:

```
...
function createPeerConnection() {
  try {
    pc = new RTCPeerConnection(pc_config, pc_constraints);

    pc.addStream(localStream);

    pc.onicecandidate = handleIceCandidate;
    console.log('Created RTCPeerConnnection with:\n' +
      ' config: \'' + JSON.stringify(pc_config) + '\';\n' +
      ' constraints: \'' + JSON.stringify(pc_constraints) + '\'.');
  } catch (e) {
    console.log('Failed to create PeerConnection, exception: ' + e.message);
    alert('Cannot create RTCPeerConnection object.');
    return;
  }

  pc.onaddstream = handleRemoteStreamAdded;
  pc.onremovestream = handleRemoteStreamRemoved;

  if (isInitiator) {
    try {
      // Create a reliable data channel
      sendChannel = pc.createDataChannel("sendDataChannel",
        {reliable: true});
      trace('Created send data channel');
    } catch (e) {
      alert('Failed to create data channel. ');
      trace('createDataChannel() failed with exception: ' + e.message);
    }
    sendChannel.onopen = handleSendChannelStateChange;
    sendChannel.onmessage = handleMessage;
    sendChannel.onclose = handleSendChannelStateChange;
  } else { // Joiner
    pc.ondatachannel = gotReceiveChannel;
  }
}
...
```

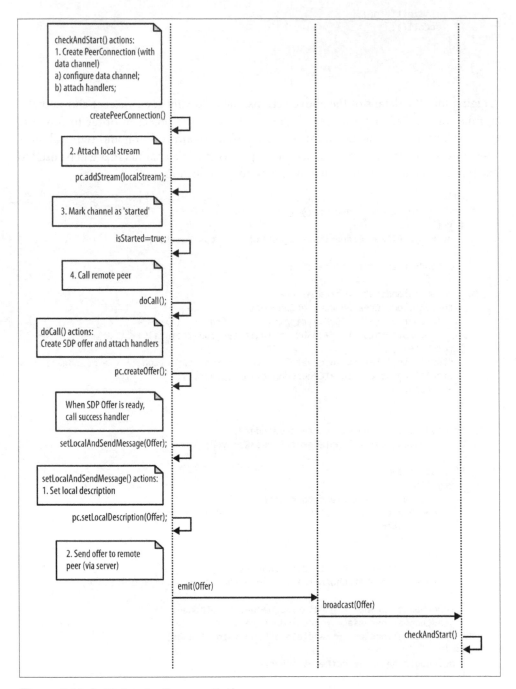

Figure 5-11. Initiator starting negotiation

With respect to the doCall() function, it basically calls the createOffer() method on the available PeerConnection, asking the browser to properly build an SDP (Session Description Protocol) object representing the Initiator's media and capabilities to be communicated to the remote party:

```
...
function doCall() {
  console.log('Creating Offer...');
  pc.createOffer(setLocalAndSendMessage,
                onSignalingError, sdpConstraints);
}
...
```

The success handler associated with this call is in charge of both associating the browser-provided SDP with the PeerConnection and transferring it to the remote peer, via the signaling server:

```
...
function setLocalAndSendMessage(sessionDescription) {
  pc.setLocalDescription(sessionDescription);
  sendMessage(sessionDescription);
}
...
```

Joiner Managing Initiator's Offer

Figure 5-12 shows the actions undertaken by the Joiner upon reception of the Initiator's SDP Offer.

Indeed, as indicated by this next JavaScript snippet, when the offer arrives at the Joiner's side, first the checkAndStart() function is run:

```
...
// Receive message from the other peer via the signalling server
socket.on('message', function (message){
  console.log('Received message:', message);
  if (message === 'got user media') {
      ...
  } else if (message.type === 'offer') {
    if (!isInitiator && !isStarted) {
      checkAndStart();
    }
    pc.setRemoteDescription(new RTCSessionDescription(message));
    doAnswer();
  } else if (message.type === 'answer' && isStarted) {
...
```

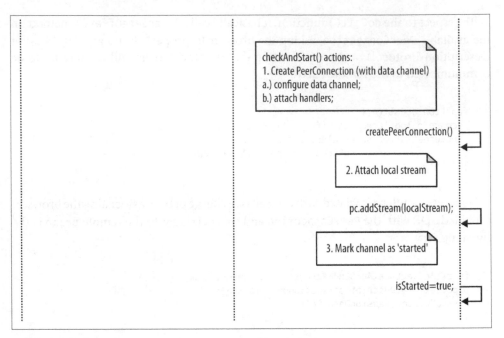

Figure 5-12. Joiner's actions after getting Initiator's Offer

When executed by the Joiner, this function creates the Joiner's `PeerConnection` object and sets the `isStarted` flag:

```
...
function checkAndStart() {

  if (!isStarted && typeof localStream != 'undefined' && isChannelReady) {
    createPeerConnection();
    isStarted = true;
    if (isInitiator) {
      ...
    }
  }
}
...
```

As will be explained in "Joiner's Answer" on page 121, once done with the `checkAndStart()` function, the Joiner still has to both configure its local `PeerConnection` and properly build the SDP Answer to be sent back to the Initiator. In the following, we will first briefly discuss the ICE candidate exchanging procedures required on both sides.

ICE Candidate Exchanging

As we already anticipated, one of the main tasks of the signaling server is to enable the exchange of network reachability information between Initiator and Joiner to make it possible to establish a flow of media packets between the two. The Interactive Connectivity Establishment (ICE), RFC5245, technique allows peers to discover enough information about each other's topology to potentially find one or more communication paths between each other.

Such information is locally gathered by the ICE Agent associated with each RTCPeer Connection object. The ICE Agent is responsible for:

- Gathering local IP, port tuple candidates
- Performing connectivity checks between peers
- Sending connection keepalives

Once a session description (either local or remote) is set, the local ICE agent automatically begins the process of discovering all of the possible candidates for the local peer:

1. The ICE agent queries the operating system for local IP addresses.
2. If configured, it queries an external STUN server to retrieve the public IP address and port tuple of the peer.
3. If configured, the agent also uses the TURN server as a last resort. If the peer-to-peer connectivity check fails, the media flow will be relayed through the TURN server.

Whenever a new candidate (i.e., IP, port tuple) is discovered, the ICE Agent automatically registers it with the RTCPeerConnection object and notifies the application via a callback function (onIceCandidate). The application can decide to transfer each candidate as soon as it is discovered (Trickle ICE) to the remote party or decide to wait for the ICE gathering phase to complete and then send all of the candidates at once.

The sequence of events associated with this specific phase is illustrated in Figure 5-13.

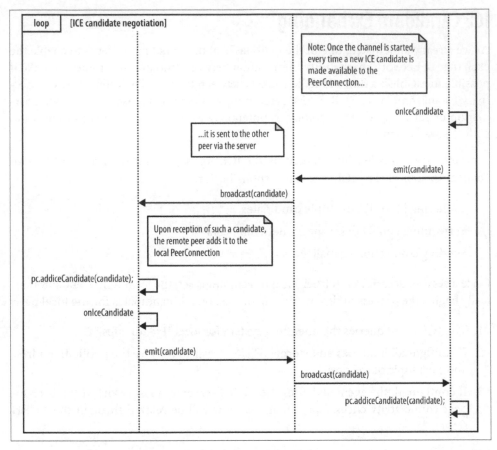

Figure 5-13. Server-mediated ICE candidate exchange procedure

The figure shows that whenever the browser raises an `IceCandidate` event (because a new ICE candidate has been gathered), the `handleIceCandidate()` handler is activated. This handler wraps the retrieved candidate inside a dedicated `candidate` message to be sent to the remote party, via the server:

```
...
function handleIceCandidate(event) {
  console.log('handleIceCandidate event: ', event);
  if (event.candidate) {
    sendMessage({
      type: 'candidate',
      label: event.candidate.sdpMLineIndex,
      id: event.candidate.sdpMid,
      candidate: event.candidate.candidate});
  } else {
    console.log('End of candidates.');
  }
```

```
}
...
```

As usual, the server simply acts as a mediator between the two negotiating parties, as witnessed by the console snapshot in Figure 5-14, which shows how the server relays both the SDP description sent by the Initiator and the ICE candidate addresses retrieved by the two interacting peers.

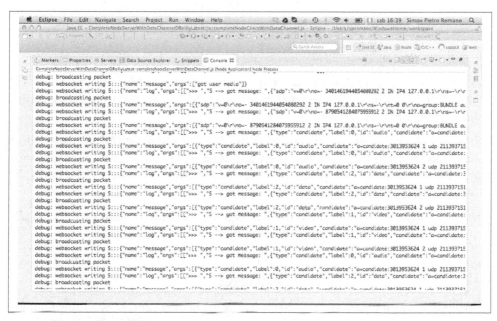

Figure 5-14. Server-mediated negotiation logs

Finally, the JavaScript snippet presented in the following indicates that the two peers add the received candidates to their own `PeerConnection` objects as soon as they arrive from the signaling server:

```javascript
...
// Receive message from the other peer via the signaling server
socket.on('message', function (message){
  console.log('Received message:', message);
  if (message === 'got user media') {
    ...
  } else if (message.type === 'offer') {
    ...
  } else if (message.type === 'answer' && isStarted) {
    ...
  } else if (message.type === 'candidate' && isStarted) {
    var candidate = new RTCIceCandidate({sdpMLineIndex:message.label,
      candidate:message.candidate});
    pc.addIceCandidate(candidate);
```

```
    } else if (message === 'bye' && isStarted) {
        ...
    }
});
...
```

Once the ICE candidates are received by the other peer, the remote session description is set on the RTCPeerConnection object (setRemoteDescription), so the ICE Agent can begin to peform the connectivity check to see if it can reach the other peer.

At this point, each ICE agent has a complete list of both its candidates and its peer's candidates. It pairs them up. To see which pairs work, each agent schedules a series of prioritized checks: local IP addresses are checked first, then public, and TURN is used as a last resort. Each check is a STUN request/response transaction that the client will perform on a particular candidate pair by sending a STUN request from the local candidate to the remote candidate.

If one of the pair candidates works, then there is a routing path for a peer-to-peer connection. Conversely, if all candidates fail, then either the RTCPeerConnection is marked as failed or the connection falls back to a TURN relay server to establish the connection.

Once a connection is established, the ICE Agent continues to issue periodic STUN requests to the other peer. This serves as a connection keepalive.

Trickle ICE

Trickle ICE is a proposed extension to the ICE protocol where instead of waiting for the ICE gathering process to complete, it is possible to send incremental updates to the other peer. This helps accelerate the overall setup phase.

The Trickle ICE mechanism involves the following steps:

- Both peers exchange SDP offers without ICE candidates.
- ICE candidates are sent via the signaling channel as soon they are discovered.
- ICE connectivity checks are run as soon as the new candidate descriptions are available.

Joiner's Answer

Now that we're done with ICE candidate exchange, let's get the train of thought back on track. We were at the point ("Joiner Managing Initiator's Offer" on page 115) where the Joiner handles Initiator's Offer by creating its own `PeerConnection` object. As sketched in Figure 5-15, once done with this, the Joiner first associates the received SDP with the newly instantiated `PeerConnection` and immediately thereafter calls the `doAnswer()` JavaScript function.

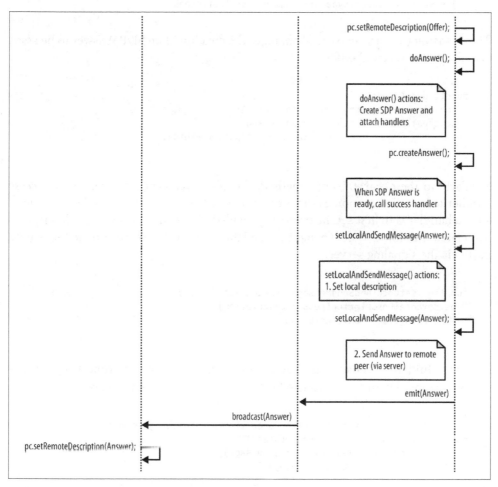

Figure 5-15. Joiner's Answer to Initiator's Offer

The snippet below highlights this specific part of the Joiner's algorithm:

```
...
// Receive message from the other peer via the signaling server
socket.on('message', function (message){
  console.log('Received message:', message);
  if (message === 'got user media') {
      ...
  } else if (message.type === 'offer') {
    ...
    pc.setRemoteDescription(new RTCSessionDescription(message));
    doAnswer();
  } else if (message.type === 'answer' && isStarted) {
...
```

The doAnswer() function basically handles the creation of an SDP Answer to be associated with the received Offer:

```
...
function doAnswer() {
  console.log('Sending answer to peer.');
  pc.createAnswer(setLocalAndSendMessage,
                  onSignalingError, sdpConstraints);
}
...
```

Similarly to the createOffer() method, the createAnswer() call sets up a success handler to be called as soon as the browser makes the local SDP available. The role of such a handler is to first set the browser-provided SDP as the local session description associated with Joiner's PeerConnection and then send such a description to the remote party via the signaling server:

```
...
function setLocalAndSendMessage(sessionDescription) {
  pc.setLocalDescription(sessionDescription);
  sendMessage(sessionDescription);
}
...
```

When the Initiator receives Joiner's Answer from the server, it can properly set it as the remote session description associated with its local PeerConnection object:

```
...
// Receive message from the other peer via the signaling server
socket.on('message', function (message){
  console.log('Received message:', message);
  if (message === 'got user media') {
      ...
  } else if (message.type === 'offer') {
      ...
  } else if (message.type === 'answer' && isStarted) {
    pc.setRemoteDescription(new RTCSessionDescription(message));
  } else if (message.type === 'candidate' && isStarted) {
```

```
    ...
} else if (message === 'bye' && isStarted) {
    ...
}
});
...
```

Going Peer-to-Peer!

We're finally all set! The two peers have successfully exchanged session descriptions and network reachability information. Two PeerConnection objects have been properly set up and configured thanks to the mediation of the signaling server. As depicted in Figure 5-16, a bidirectional multimedia communication channel is now available as a direct transport means between the two browsers. The server is now done with its task and will be from now on completely bypassed by the two communicating peers.

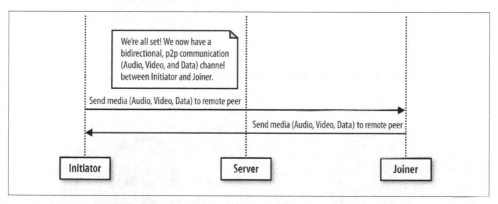

Figure 5-16. Going peer-to-peer after communication setup

The two snapshots in Figures 5-17 and 5-18 show, respectively, the Joiner's and the Initiator's windows right after successful channel negotiation. You can see in both figures that each peer now has available local and remote views, as well as two text areas that can be used, respectively, to send direct messages to the remote party and to log direct messages received from the remote party.

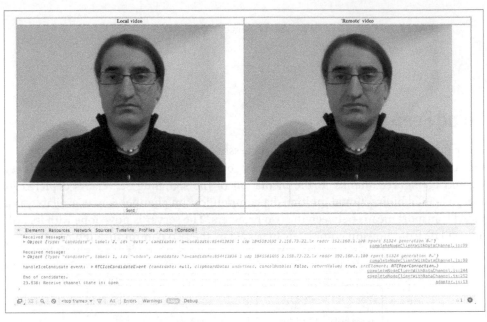

Figure 5-17. Communication established in Chrome: Joiner's side

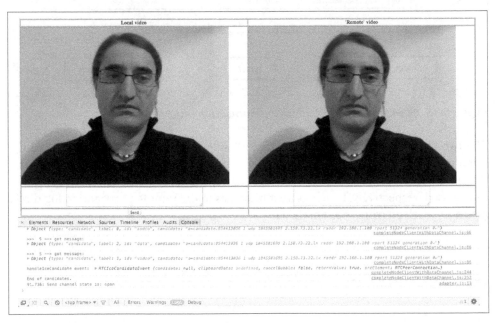

Figure 5-18. Communication established in Chrome: Initiator's side

Using the Data Channel

In this subsection we will delve into the details of configuring and using the data channel. Actually, the data channel is created by the Initiator as part of the `createPeerConnection()` function code:

```
...
function createPeerConnection() {
  try {
    pc = new RTCPeerConnection(pc_config, pc_constraints);
    ...
  } catch (e) {
    ...
  }
  pc.onaddstream = handleRemoteStreamAdded;
  pc.onremovestream = handleRemoteStreamRemoved;

  if (isInitiator) {
    try {
      // Create a reliable data channel
      sendChannel = pc.createDataChannel("sendDataChannel",
                                          {reliable: true});
      trace('Created send data channel');
    } catch (e) {
      ...
    }
    sendChannel.onopen = handleSendChannelStateChange;
    sendChannel.onmessage = handleMessage;
    sendChannel.onclose = handleSendChannelStateChange;
  } else { // Joiner
    pc.ondatachannel = gotReceiveChannel;
  }
}
...
```

The above snippet shows how a number of handlers are associated with the data channel. As an example, we present below the `handleSendChannelStateChange()` function, which takes care of enabling both the sender's text area and the Send button as soon as the channel reaches the open state:

```
...
function handleSendChannelStateChange() {
  var readyState = sendChannel.readyState;
  trace('Send channel state is: ' + readyState);
  if (readyState == "open") {
    dataChannelSend.disabled = false;
    dataChannelSend.focus();
    dataChannelSend.placeholder = "";
    sendButton.disabled = false;
  } else {
    dataChannelSend.disabled = true;
    sendButton.disabled = true;
```

```
    }
  }
  ...
```

The sendData() JavaScript function shown below is configured as a handler for the Send button and performs the following actions: (1) it collects text inserted by the user in the sendTextArea; and (2) it sends such text across the instantiated data channel.

```
...
// Handler associated with Send button
sendButton.onclick = sendData;
...
function sendData() {
  var data = sendTextarea.value;
  if(isInitiator) sendChannel.send(data);
  else receiveChannel.send(data);
  trace('Sent data: ' + data);
}
...
```

Figure 5-19 shows the Initiator's window right after having sent a text message across the data channel.

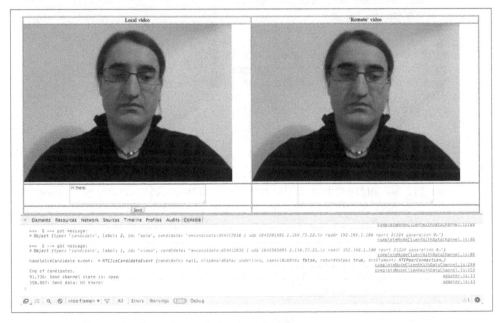

Figure 5-19. Using the data channel: Initiator's side

Once the message arrives at the other side, the handleMessage() function is triggered. This function, which is shown below, simply takes the transferred data and logs them inside the receiveTextArea element of the HTML page:

```
...
function handleMessage(event) {
  trace('Received message: ' + event.data);
  receiveTextarea.value += event.data + '\n';
}
...
```

This is also shown in the snapshot contained in Figure 5-20.

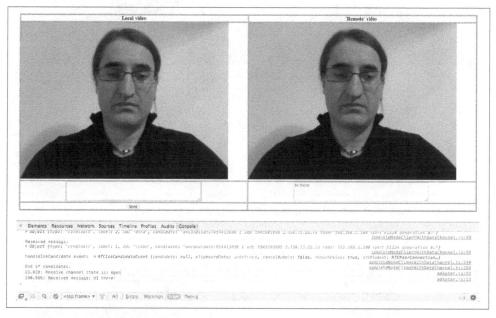

Figure 5-20. Using the data channel: Joiner's side

Moving on to the receive channel, as soon as Joiner's browser raises the dataChannel event, the gotReceiveChannel() function is activated. This handler sets up the receive channel and properly configures it for the management of channel-related events:

```
...
function gotReceiveChannel(event) {
  trace('Receive Channel Callback');
  receiveChannel = event.channel;
  receiveChannel.onmessage = handleMessage;
  receiveChannel.onopen = handleReceiveChannelStateChange;
  receiveChannel.onclose = handleReceiveChannelStateChange;
}
...
```

Figures 5-21 and 5-22 show, respectively, the Joiner sending back an answer to the Initiator across the data channel and the Initiator receiving the answer and logging it inside the data channel text area.

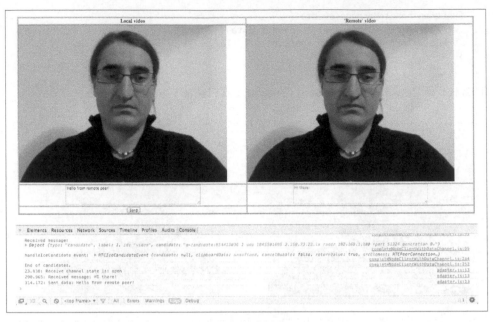

Figure 5-21. Data channel: Joiner answering Initiator's message

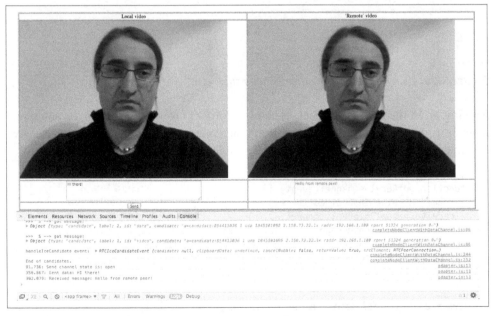

Figure 5-22. Data channel: Initiator getting Joiner's answer

A Quick Look at the Chrome WebRTC Internals Tool

In this last section, we will provide some information about the WebRTC-specific debugging tools made available by Google Chrome. Indeed, when you're using a WebRTC-enabled web application, you can monitor its status by opening a new tab and entering *chrome://webrtc-internals/* inside the tab's location bar. For the case of our sample application, a snapshot of the *webrtc-internals* tab is presented in Figure 5-23.

WebRTC Internals

▶ Create Dump

PeerConnection 71221-1

PeerConnection 71229-1

Figure 5-23. Active PeerConnections

As shown in the figure, the logging page reports information about the active `PeerConnection` objects. In our case, since we're running both the Initiator and the Joiner on the same machine, we see two active `PeerConnection` instances, associated, respectively, with the Initiator (`PeerConnection71221-1`) and with the Joiner (`PeerConnection71229-1`). By clicking on one of the reported identifiers, fine-grained information about the related `PeerConnection` appears. As an example, Figures 5-24 and 5-25 show, respectively, the Initiator's Offer and corresponding Joiner's Answer in the form of SDP objects. In the same figures, you can also see a list of all events generated by the browser while processing the call.

Figure 5-24. The SDP Offer

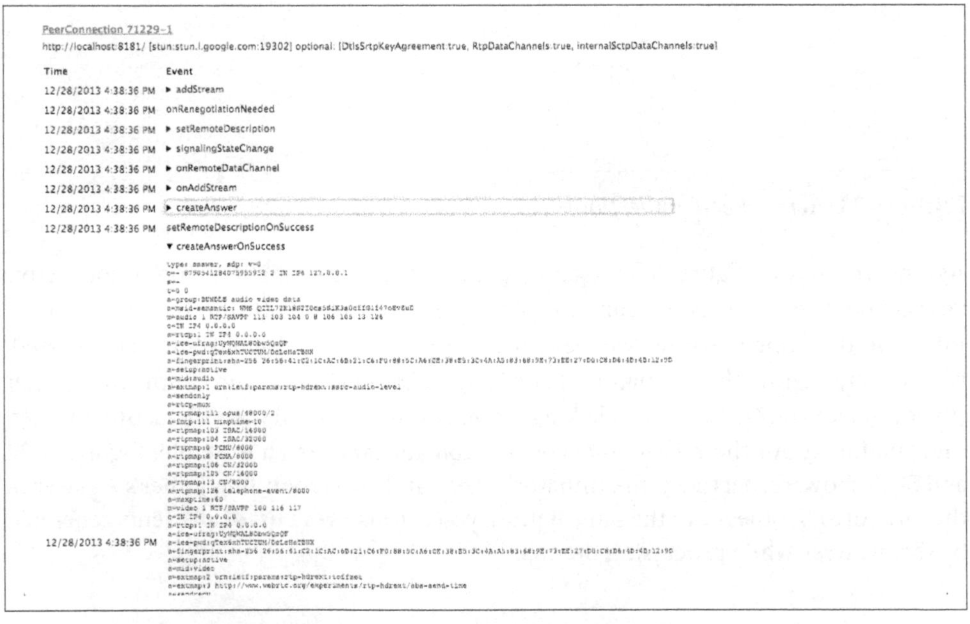

Figure 5-25. The SDP Answer

Chrome is also very good at reporting channel statistics for all of the media involved in a peer-to-peer exchange. As an example, you can see in Figure 5-26 that channel information (channel creation timestamp, browser component handling the channel, local and remote channel certificates for secure information exchanging) is reported for audio, video, and data channels.

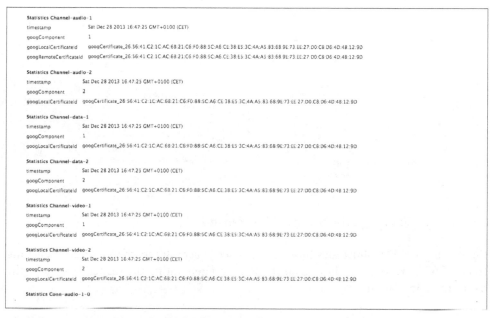

Figure 5-26. Channel statistics in text format

Figure 5-27 instead reports, in graphical format, detailed information about both network-related (estimated available bandwidth, packets sent per second, average round-trip time, etc.) and encoding-related (target encoding bit rate, actual encoding bit rate, etc.) information about media (i.e., both audio and video) streams.

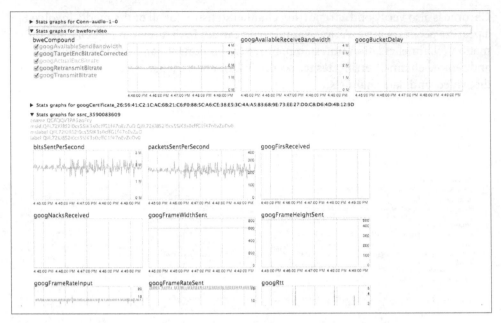

Figure 5-27. Channel statistics in graphical format

Finally, Figure 5-28 illustrates how the browser is actually in charge of both keeping track of ICE protocol machine state changes and generating the related events for the overlying application.

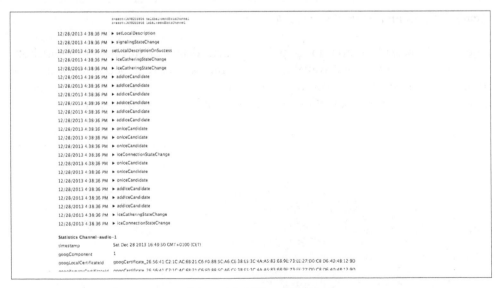

Figure 5-28. Signaling state machine with ICE candidate events

CHAPTER 6

An Introduction to WebRTC API's Advanced Features

In the previous chapters, we described and discussed a simple scenario: a browser talking directly to another browser. The WebRTC APIs are designed around the one-to-one communication scenario, which represents the easiest to manage and deploy. As we illustrated in previous chapters, the basic WebRTC features are sufficient to implement the one-to-one scenario since the built-in audio and video engines of the browser are responsible for optimizing the delivery of the media streams by adapting them to match the available bandwidth and to fit the current network conditions.

In this last chapter we will briefly talk about the conferencing scenario and then list other advanced WebRTC features and mechanisms that are still under active discussion and development within the W3C WebRTC working group (at the time of writing in early 2014).

Conferencing

In a WebRTC conferencing scenario (or *N-way* call), each browser has to receive and handle the media streams generated by the other N-1 browsers, as well as deliver its own generated media streams to N-1 browsers (i.e., the application-level topology is a mesh network). While this is a quite straightforward scenario, it is nonetheless difficult to manage for a browser and at the same time calls for linearly increasing network bandwidth availability.

For these reasons, video conferencing systems usually rely upon a *star topology* where each peer connects to a dedicated server that is simultaneously responsible for:

- Negotiating parameters with every other peer in the network
- Controlling conferencing resources

- Aggregating (or *mixing*) the individual streams
- Distributing the proper mixed stream to each and every peer participating in the conference

Delivering a single stream clearly reduces both the amount of bandwidth and amount of CPU (and possibly GPU [Graphics Processing Unit]) resources required by each peer involved in a conference. The dedicated server can be either one of the peers or a server specifically optimized for processing and distributing real-time data. In the latter case, the server is usually identified as a *Multipoint Control Unit (MCU)*.

The WebRTC API does not provide any particular mechanism to assist the conferencing scenario. The criteria and process to identify the MCU are delegated to the application. However, this is a big engineering challenge because it envisages the introduction of a centralized infrastructure in the WebRTC peer-to-peer communication model. The upside of such a challenge clearly resides in the consideration that being capable of establishing a peer connection with a proxy server adds to the benefits offered by WebRTC through the additional services offered by the proxy server itself.

We plan to dedicate at least one chapter to videoconferencing in the next version of this book.

Identity and Authentication

The DTLS handshake performed between two WebRTC browsers relies on self-signed certificates. Hence, such certificates cannot be used to also authenticate the peers as there is no explicit chain of trust.

The W3C WebRTC working group is actually working on a web-based *Identity Provider (IdP)* mechanism. The idea is that each browser has a relationship with an IdP supporting a protocol (for example, *OpenId* or *BrowserID*) that can be used to assert its own identity when interacting with the other peers. The interaction with the IdP is designed in such a way as to decouple the browser from any particular Identity Provider (i.e., each browser involved in the communication might have relationships with different IdPs).

 The `setIdentityProvider()` method sets the Identity Provider to be used for a given `PeerConnection` object. Applications do not need to invoke this call if the browser is already configured for a specific IdP. In this case, the configured IdP will be used to get an assertion.

The browser sending the Offer acts as the *Authenticating Party (AP)* and obtains from the IdP an *Identity Assertion* binding its identity to its own fingerprint (generated during the DTLS handshake). This identity assertion is then attached to the Offer.

The `getIdentityProvider()` method initiates the process of obtaining an Identity Assertion. Applications do not need to invoke this call; the method is merely intended to allow them to start the process of obtaining Identity Assertions before a call is initiated.

The browser playing the role of the consumer during the Offer/Answer exchange phase (for instance, the one with the `RTCPeerConnection` on which `setRemoteDescription()` is called) acts as the *Relying Party (RP)* and verifies the assertion by directly contacting the IdP of the browser sending the Offer (Figure 6-1). When using the Chrome browser, this allows the consumer to display a *trusted* icon indicating that a call is coming in from a trusted contact.

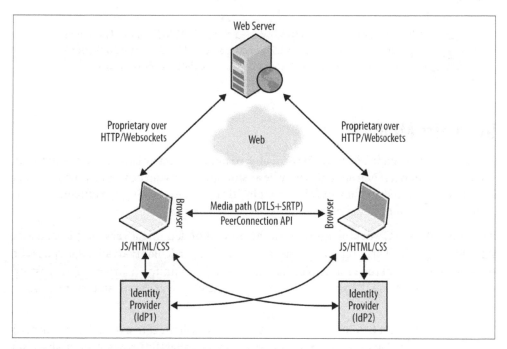

Figure 6-1. A WebRTC call with IdP-based identity

Peer-to-Peer DTMF

Dual-Tone Multi-Frequency (DTMF) signaling is an encoding technique used in telephony systems to encode numeric codes in the form of sound signals in the audio band between telephone handsets (as well as other communication devices) and the switching center. As an example, DTMF is used to navigate through an *Interactive Voice Responder* (IVR).

In order to send DTMF (for example, through the phone keypad) values across an RTCPeerConnection, the user agent needs to know which specific MediaStreamTrack will carry the tone.

The createDTMFSender() method creates an RTCDTMFSender object that references the given MediaStreamTrack. The MediaStream Track must be an element of a MediaStream that is currently in the RTCPeerConnection object's local streams set.

Once an RTCDTMFSender object has been created, it can be used to send DTMF tones across that MediaStreamTrack (over the PeerConnection) through the insertDTMF() method.

The insertDTMF() method is used to send DTMF tones. The tones parameter is treated as a series of characters. The characters *0* through *9*, *A* through *D*, *#*, and *** generate the associated DTMF tones.

Statistics Model

A real-time communication framework also requires a mechanism to extract statistics on its performance. Such statistics may be as simple as knowing how many bytes of data have been delivered, or they may be as sophisiticated as measuring the efficiency of an echo canceller on the local device.

The W3C WebRTC working group is in the process of defining a very simple statistics API, whereby a call may return all relevant data for a particular MediaStreamTrack, or for the PeerConnection as a whole. Statistical data has a uniform structure, consisting of a string identifying the specific statistics parameter and an associated simple-typed value.

Providers of this API (such as the different browsers) will use it to expose both standard and nonstandard statistics. The basic statistics model is that the browser maintains a set of statistics referenced by a selector. The selector may, for example, be a specific Media StreamTrack. For a track to be a valid selector, it must be a member of a MediaStream that is either sent or received across the RTCPeerConnection object on which the stats request was issued.

The calling web application provides the selector to the getStats() method and the browser emits a set of statistics that it believes is relevant to such a selector.

The getStats() method gathers statistics for the given selector and reports the result asynchronously.

More precisely, the getStats() method takes a valid selector (e.g., a MediaStream Track) as input, along with a callback to be executed when the stats are available. The callback is given an RTCStatsReport containing RTCStats objects. An RTCStatsRe port object represents a map associating strings (identifying the inspected objects— *RTCStats.id*) with their corresponding RTCStats containers.

An RTCStatsReport may be composed of several RTCStats objects, each reporting stats for one underlying object that the implementation thinks is relevant for the selector. The former collects global information associated with the selector by summing up all the stats of a certain type. For instance, if a MediaStreamTrack is carried by multiple SSRCs over the network, the RTCStatsReport may contain one RTCStats object per SSRC (which can be distinguished by the value of the ssrc stats attribute).

The statistics returned are designed in such a way that repeated queries can be linked by the RTCStats id dictionary member (see Table 6-1). Thus, a web application can measure performance over a given time period by requesting measurements both at its beginning and at its end.

Table 6-1. RTCStats dictionary members

Member	Type	Description
id	DOMString	A unique id that is associated with the object that was inspected to produce this RTCStats object.
timestamp	DOMHiResTimeStamp	The timestamp, of type DOMHiResTimeStamp [HIGHRES-TIME], associated with this object. The time is relative to the UNIX epoch (Jan 1, 1970, UTC).
type	RTCStatsType	The type of this object.

Currently, the only defined types are inbound-rtp and outbound-rtp, both of which are instances of the RTCRTPStreamStats subclass that additionally provides remoteId and ssrc properties:

- The outbound-rtp object type is represented by the subclass RTCOutboundRTP StreamStats, providing packetsSent and bytesSent properties.

- The inbound-rtp object type is represented by the subclass RTCInboundRTPStream Stats, providing analogous packetsReceived and bytesReceived properties.

WebRTC 1.0 APIs

This Appendix provides a summary of the W3C WebRTC APIs.

RTCPeerConnection API

An RTCPeerConnection allows two users to communicate directly, browser to browser.

Configuration

Table A-1. RTCConfiguration dictionary members

Name	Type	Default	Description
iceServers	sequence<RTCIceServer>		An array containing URIs of servers available to be used by ICE, such as STUN and TURN servers.
iceTransports	RTCIceTransports	"all"	Indicates which candidates the ICE engine is allowed to use.
requestIdentity	RTCIdentityOption	"ifconfigured"	See the requestIdentity member of the RTCOfferAnswerOptions dictionary.

Table A-2. RTCIceServer dictionary members

Name	Type	Description
credential	DOMString	If this RTCIceServer object represents a TURN server, then this attribute specifies the credentials to use with that TURN server.
urls	(DOMString or sequence <DOMString>)	STUN or TURN URI(s) as defined in [STUN-URI] and [TURN-URI] or other URI types
username	DOMString	If this RTCIceServer object represents a TURN server, then this attribute specifies the username to use with that TURN server.

Table A-3. RTCIceTransports enumeration values

Value	Description
none	The ICE engine must not send or receive any packets at this point.
relay	The ICE engine must only use media relay candidates such as candidates passing through a TURN server. This can be used to reduce leakage of IP addresses in certain use cases.
all	The ICE engine may use any type of candidates when this value is specified.

Constructor

This is the RTCPeerConnection constructor:

- **RTCPeerConnection**(*configuration*)

Methods

Here are the RTCPeerConnection methods:

- createOffer (**RTCSessionDescriptionCallback** *successCallback*, **RTCPeerConnectionErrorCallback** *failureCallback*, optional **RTCOfferOptions** *options*)|
- createAnswer (**RTCSessionDescriptionCallback** *successCallback*, **RTCPeerConnectionErrorCallback** *failureCallback*, optional **RTCOfferAnswerOptions** *options*)
- setLocalDescription (**RTCSessionDescription** *description*, VoidFunction *successCallback*, **RTCPeerConnectionErrorCallback** *failureCallback*)
- setRemoteDescription (**RTCSessionDescription** *description*, VoidFunction *successCallback*, **RTCPeerConnectionErrorCallback** *failureCallback*)
- updateIce (**RTCConfiguration** *configuration*)
- addIceCandidate (**RTCIceCandidate** *candidate*, VoidFunction *successCallback*, **RTCPeerConnectionErrorCallback** *failureCallback*)
- getConfiguration ()
- getLocalStreams ()
- getRemoteStreams ()
- getStreamById (DOMString *streamId*)
- addStream (MediaStream *stream*)
- removeStream (MediaStream *stream*)
- close ()

Attributes

Table A-4. RTCPeerConnection attributes

Access property	Type	Name
readonly	RTCSessionDescription	remoteDescription
readonly	RTCSignalingState	signalingState
readonly	RTCIceGatheringState	iceGatheringState
readonly	RTCIceConnectionState	iceConnectionState
	EventHandler	onnegotiationneeded
	EventHandler	onicecandidate
	EventHandler	onsignalingstatechange
	EventHandler	onaddstream
	EventHandler	onremovestream
	EventHandler	oniceconnectionstatechange

State Definition

Table A-5. RTCSignalingState

Value	Description
stable	There is no offer/answer exchange in progress. This is also the initial state in which case the local and remote descriptions are empty.
have-local-offer	A local description, of type "offer," has been successfully applied.
have-remote-offer	A remote description, of type "offer," has been successfully applied.
have-local-pranswer	A remote description of type "offer" has been successfully applied and a local description of type "pranswer" has been successfully applied.
have-remote-pranswer	A local description of type "offer" has been successfully applied and a remote description of type "pranswer" has been successfully applied.
closed	The connection is closed.

Table A-6. RTCIceGatheringState

Value	Description
new	The object was just created, and no networking has occurred yet.
gathering	The ICE engine is in the process of gathering candidates for this RTCPeerConnection.
complete	The ICE engine has completed gathering. Events such as adding a new interface or a new TURN server will cause the state to go back to gathering.

Table A-7. RTCIceConnectionState

Value	Description
new	The ICE Agent is gathering addresses and/or waiting for remote candidates to be supplied.
checking	The ICE Agent has received remote candidates on at least one component, and is checking candidate pairs but has not yet found a connection. In addition to checking, it may also still be gathering.
connected	The ICE Agent has found a usable connection for all components but is still checking other candidate pairs to see if there is a better connection. It may also still be gathering.
completed	The ICE Agent has finished gathering and checking and found a connection for all components.
failed	The ICE Agent is finished checking all candidate pairs and failed to find a connection for at least one component. Connections may have been found for some components.
disconnected	Liveness checks have failed for one or more components. This is more aggressive than failed, and may trigger intermittently (and resolve itself without action) on a flaky network.
closed	The ICE Agent has shut down and is no longer responding to STUN requests.

Peer-to-Peer Data API

The Peer-to-Peer Data API lets a web application send and receive generic application data peer-to-peer. The API for sending and receiving data models the behavior of WebSockets.

- Method:
  RTCDataChannel
    createDataChannel ([TreatNullAs=EmptyString] DOMString label, optional **RTCDataChannelInit** dataChannelDict)

- Attribute:
  EventHandler
    ondatachannel

Interface RTCDataChannel Interface Methods

Table A-8. Methods

Return type	Name
void	close()
void	send(DOMString data)
void	send(Blob data)
void	send(ArrayBuffer data)
void	send(ArrayBufferView data)

RTCDataChannel Interface Attributes

Table A-9. Attributes

Access property	Type	Name
readonly	DOMString	label
readonly	boolean	ordered
readonly	unsigned?	maxRetransmitTime
readonly	unsigned?	maxRetransmits
readonly	DOMString	protocol
readonly	attribute	negotiated
readonly	unsigned short	id
readonly	RTCDataChannelState	readyState
readonly	unsigned long	bufferedAmount
	EventHandler	onopen
	EventHandler	onerror
	EventHandler	onclose
	EventHandler	onmessage
	DOMString	binaryType

Table A-10. RTCDataChannelInit dictionary

Name	Type	Description
id	unsigned short	Overrides the default selection of ID for this channel.
maxRetransmitTime	unsigned short	Limits the time during which the channel will retransmit data if not successfully delivered.
maxRetransmits	unsigned short	Limits the number of times a channel will retransmit data if not successfully delivered.
negotiated	boolean	Defaults to false. The default value of false tells the user agent to announce the channel in-band and instruct the other peer to dispatch a corresponding RTCData Channel object. If set to true, it is up to the application to negotiate the channel and create an RTCDataChannel object with the same ID as the other peer.
ordered	boolean	Defaults to true. If set to false, data is allowed to be delivered out of order. The default value of true guarantees that data will be delivered in order.
protocol	DOMString	Defaults to "". Subprotocol name used for this channel.

Table A-11. RTCDataChannelState enumeration values

Value	Description
connecting	The user agent is attempting to establish the underlying data transport. This is the initial state of an RTCData Channel object created with createDataChannel().
open	The underlying data transport is established and communication is possible. This is the initial state of an RTCDa taChannel object dispatched as a part of an RTCDataChannelEvent.
closing	The procedure to close down the underlying data transport has started.
closed	The underlying data transport has been closed or could not be established.

Index

We'd like to hear your suggestions for improving our indexes. Send email to index@oreilly.com.

setIdentityProvider() method, 134
setLocalDescription() method, 40
setRemoteDescription() method, 40
RTCSessionDescription API, 40
RTCStats API, 137
RTCStatsReport API, 137
RTP Control Protocol (RTCP), 7

S

SCTP (Stream Control Transmission Protocol), 8
SDP (Session Description Protocol), 5, 115
Secure Real-time Transport Protocol (SRTP), 7
security
    DTLS, 6
    identity and authentication, 134–135
send() method, RTCDataChannel, 57
Session Description Protocol (see SDP)
session descriptions, 5
    (see also JSEP; SDP)
Session Initiation Protocol (SIP), 2
Session Traversal Utilities for NAT (see STUN)
setIdentityProvider() method, RTCPeerConnection, 134
setLocalDescription() method, RTCPeerConnection, 40
setRemoteDescription() method, RTCPeerConnection, 40
signaling, 5, 9, 25–26, 63, 113
    call flow for, 63–72, 91–95
    channel initiator, 65, 104–110
    channel joiner, 65, 76–78, 110–112, 121–122
    closing channel, 85–88
    continuing conversation, 82–84
    creating channel, 72–75
    DTMF, 135–136
    signaling server, 65
    starting conversation, 79–81, 112–122
sinks, media, 19
SIP (Session Initiation Protocol), 2
socket.io library, 66
sources, media, 19
SRTP (Secure Real-time Transport Protocol), 7
star topology, 133
statistics model, 136–137
stop() method, LocalMediaStream, 6
Stream Control Transmission Protocol (see SCTP)

STUN (Session Traversal Utilities for NAT), 8, 37

T

TLS (Transport Layer Security), 6
Trapezoid model, 2
Traversal Using Relays around NAT (see TURN)
Triangle model, 2–3
Trickle ICE, 120
TURN (Traversal Using Relays around NAT), 8, 37

U

UDP (User Datagram Protocol), 6
URI (Uniform Resource Identifier), 1
URL (Uniform Resource Locator), 1
    blob URL, 13, 18
    unique, creating, 13
User Datagram Protocol (see UDP)

V

video codecs, 6
video conferencing, 133–134
video stream (see MediaStream API)

W

W3C (World Wide Web Consortium)
    Media Capture and Streams API, 12–13
    statistics API, 136
    WebRTC-related standards, 1
web architecture, 1–3
web browsers, 12
    (see also specific browsers)
    media sources and sinks, 19
    peer-to-peer communication between, 2–4
WebRTC (Web Real-Time Communication), vii, 1
    application call flow, 91–95
    application example, 95–104
    architecture, 2–3
    browsers supporting, 12
    conferencing, 133–134
    identity and authentication, 134–135
    peer-to-peer communication, 2–4, 123–127
    protocol stack, 8
    signaling, 5, 9, 25–26

About the Authors

Salvatore Loreto, PhD and MBA (ongoing), works as a senior researcher for Ericsson Research in Finland. He is involved in standardization, research projects, and strategy related to the Internet in general (in particular, VoIP, web communication, and machine-to-machine [M2M] technologies). He has been active in IETF since 2000, where he has coauthored several RFCs; and serves as co-chair for several working groups in the Application and Real-Time Application areas. He is coauthoring the WebRTC data-channel-related drafts. He is also a senior member of IEEE and serves as Associate Technical Editor for *IEEE Communication Magazine* and the *IEEE Internet of Things* journal.

Simon Pietro Romano is both a university professor and a startupper. He teaches Computer Networks and Telematics Applications at the University of Napoli "Federico II." He is the cofounder of Meetecho, a startup and University spin-off dealing with WebRTC-based unified collaboration. He actively participates in IETF standardization activities, mainly in the Real-Time Application and Infrastructure (RAI) area.

Colophon

The animal on the cover of *Real-Time Communication with WebRTC* is the viviparous lizard (*Zootoca vivipara*), also known as the common lizard and scaly lizard. It is found throughout most of Europe and Asia, in one of the widest ranges of any vertebrate. *Viviparous* is a term applied to animals who birth live offspring, and indeed, these lizards have the ability to carry and deliver fully formed young. Interestingly, this seems to be an adaptation made solely for cool climates, as populations of this species in warmer areas like Spain and Italy lay eggs instead.

While the southern and northern populations of viviparous lizards also prefer slightly different types of habitat (for instance, the southern lizards can be found at higher elevations and in damper environments), they all live on the ground and spend their time eating small insects and basking in the sun to maintain body temperature. Northern lizards also hibernate from September to mid-February, while their southern cousins are active all year.

The viviparous lizard averages 13-15 centimeters long. Males have larger heads, more slender bodies, and colored underbellies, while females are much duller in color. As a species, however, their coloration varies a great deal. Most often, the lizards are brown with darker markings on their back and legs, but can also be green, gray, black, or red —which can make it difficult to identify them. It is quite likely that viviparous lizards should be reclassified into multiple subspecies, but this work has not yet been completed.

The cover image is from Wood's *Animate Creation*. The cover fonts are URW Typewriter and Guardian Sans. The text font is Adobe Minion Pro; the heading font is Adobe Myriad Condensed; and the code font is Dalton Maag's Ubuntu Mono.

Have it your way.

O'Reilly eBooks

- Lifetime access to the book when you buy through oreilly.com
- Provided in up to four DRM-free file formats, for use on the devices of your choice: PDF, .epub, Kindle-compatible .mobi, and Android .apk
- Fully searchable, with copy-and-paste and print functionality
- Alerts when files are updated with corrections and additions

oreilly.com/ebooks/

Safari Books Online

- Access the contents and quickly search over 7000 books on technology, business, and certification guides
- Learn from expert video tutorials, and explore thousands of hours of video on technology and design topics
- Download whole books or chapters in PDF format, at no extra cost, to print or read on the go
- Get early access to books as they're being written
- Interact directly with authors of upcoming books
- Save up to 35% on O'Reilly print books

See the complete Safari Library at safari.oreilly.com

O'REILLY®

Spreading the knowledge of innovators.   oreilly.com

Get even more for your money.

Join the O'Reilly Community, and register the O'Reilly books you own. It's free, and you'll get:

- $4.99 ebook upgrade offer
- 40% upgrade offer on O'Reilly print books
- Membership discounts on books and events
- Free lifetime updates to ebooks and videos
- Multiple ebook formats, DRM FREE
- Participation in the O'Reilly community
- Newsletters
- Account management
- 100% Satisfaction Guarantee

Signing up is easy:

1. **Go to: oreilly.com/go/register**
2. **Create an O'Reilly login.**
3. **Provide your address.**
4. **Register your books.**

Note: English-language books only

To order books online:
oreilly.com/store

For questions about products or an order:
orders@oreilly.com

To sign up to get topic-specific email announcements and/or news about upcoming books, conferences, special offers, and new technologies:
elists@oreilly.com

For technical questions about book content:
booktech@oreilly.com

To submit new book proposals to our editors:
proposals@oreilly.com

O'Reilly books are available in multiple DRM-free ebook formats. For more information:
oreilly.com/ebooks

O'REILLY®

Spreading the knowledge of innovators   oreilly.com

9 781449 371876